JANE MILLS

Jane Mills is Associate Professor of Communication in the School of Communication and Creative Industries at Charles Sturt University and the Series Editor of Australian Screen Classics. She has a production background in journalism, radio, television and documentary film, and has written and broadcast widely on cinema, censorship, feminism, sociolinguistics and human rights. Her current research interests concern screen literacy and Geocriticism and her recent books include *The Money Shot: Cinema, Sin and Censorship* and *Loving and Hating Hollywood: Reframing Global and Local Cinemas*.

In memory of John Carroll,
a much loved and admired mentor, colleague and friend.

jedda

JANE MILLS

First published by Currency Press Pty Ltd and the NFSA in 2012.

Currency Press Pty Ltd
PO Box 2287, Strawberry Hills
NSW 2012 Australia
enquiries@currency.com.au
www.currency.com.au

National Film and Sound Archive
GPO Box 2002, Canberra
ACT 2601 Australia
www.nfsa.afc.gov.au

Australian Screen Classics series: ISSN 1447-557X

National Library of Australia—Cataloguing-in-Publication Data:

Author:	Mills, Jane.
Title:	Jedda / Jane Mills.
ISBN:	9780868199207 (pbk.)
Series:	Australian screen classics
Notes:	Includes bibliographical references.
Subjects:	Jedda (Motion picture). Motion pictures, Australian.
	Feature films—Australia—History and criticism.
Dewey Number:	791.4372

Cover design by Katy Wall for Currency Press
Typeset by Katy Wall for Currency Press in Iowan Old Style roman 9.5 pt.
Printed by Hyde Park Press, Richmond SA
All images within the text are reproduced with the kind permission of Richard Chauvel Carlsson.

AUSTRALIAN SCREEN CLASSICS

JANE MILLS
Series Editor

Our national cinema plays a vital role in our cultural heritage and in showing us at least something of what it is to be Australian. But the picture can get blurred by unruly forces such as competing artistic aims, inconstant personal tastes, political vagaries, constantly changing priorities in screen education and training, technological innovation and the market.

When these forces remain unconnected, the result can be an artistically impoverished cinema and audiences who are disinclined to seek out and derive pleasure from a diverse range of films, including Australian ones.

This series is a part of screen culture which is the glue needed to stick these forces together. It's the plankton in the moving image food chain that feeds the imagination of our filmmakers and their audiences. It's what makes sense of the opinions, memories, responses, knowledge and exchange of ideas about film.

Above all, screen culture is informed by a love of cinema. And it has to be carefully nurtured if we are to understand and appreciate the aesthetic, moral, intellectual and sentient value of our national cinema.

Australian Screen Classics will match some of our best-loved films with some of our most distinguished writers and thinkers, drawn from the worlds of culture, criticism and politics. All we ask of our writers is that they feel passionate about the films they choose. Through these thoughtful, elegantly-written books, we hope that screen culture will work its sticky magic and introduce more audiences to Australian cinema.

Jane Mills is Associate Professor in Communication in the School of Communication and Creative Industries at Charles Sturt University.

CONTENTS

ACKNOWLEDGMENTS

The last thing a publisher needs is for an author to give up. This time, however, I was not altogether unhappy when an author confessed he was unable to deliver his manuscript for this series. To fill the gap in our publishing schedule I volunteered to write about *Jedda*, a film I had wanted to write about for many years. My initial concern about whether it was seemly for the Series Editor to commission herself was laid to rest by the publishers at Currency Press and the National Film & Sound Archive. As Graham Shirley, the Archive's Film Historian, pointed out, it is not uncommon in our industry for producers and directors to write or direct an episode in a television series or a short film in a compilation movie. So thank you, Graham, for putting my mind at rest and for all the support and advice you have generously given to many of our authors.

My thanks to publishers Victoria Chance, Deborah Franco and Paul O'Beirne at Currency Press and David Boden at the NFSA for their confidence in me. As ever, my thanks to Simon Drake, also at the NFSA, for his help on this and all previous titles. Once again, my sincere thanks to Sarah Shrubb whose editorial skills and understanding are unsurpassed. And a big thank you to the librarians of the Australian Film, Television and Radio School, whose support and commitment to screen culture is unparalleled.

I wish to acknowledge the Arts Faculty Research Office of Charles Sturt University for awarding me a grant that enabled me to explore how my understanding of cinema might be informed by visiting the film's locations.

For their warm hospitality in the Northern Territory, my sincere thanks to: Kristina Jones at Coolibah Station; Jason Grey, my inspired tour guide at Nitmiluk; the owners or managers of the motels and camp sites on the Victoria River, in Darwin, Katherine, Mataranka, Tennant Creek and Alice Springs. I offer special thanks to Shelagh and Colin O'Brien at the Glen Helen Resort, who yet again made me welcome and helped me locate the exact place where one particular shot was filmed. The publishers join me in my sincere thanks to Ric Chauvel Carlsson for his generosity in giving us permission for the illustrations.

Jedda has been widely written about, and both loved and hated by numerous critics and audiences. Of all these, I'd like to single out Stuart Cunningham, whose ideas in his book, *Featuring Australia: The Cinema of Charles Chauvel*, proved to be an invaluable guide. I thank Maree Delofski for first introducing *Jedda* to me, Sylvia Lawson for her continuing support over the years, and Jane Stadler, who shares my desire to locate locations and whose own footsteps in those of the *Jedda* cast and crew I followed. Lastly, my love and thanks to David McKnight, whose advice is always welcome and always listened to.

Finally, if the author who for very understandable reasons dropped out is reading this, I hope you eventually write the book I had been looking forward to publishing. Please don't give up.

Jedda and Marbuk.

INTRODUCTION

Lost on location

Even though I know exactly where I am, I feel lost. I am standing in a vast valley; it is a little before midday, the sun is getting hotter by the minute, the gusts of wind are too warm for comfort, and the dusty air threatens to choke me. All around the land is flat and red; the tall grass bleached white by the sun. There are wire fences, a track stretching out in front and disappearing over a saddle between two high ridges, a few skinny palm trees, and some stunted, scrubby-looking gums. I can see hundreds—no, thousands—of bizarrely shaped, dark red anthills that assume human forms: here is a finger pointing to the sky, there a Madonna and child, and everywhere bulbous penises. In the distance, two high ridges force me to look up at their towering profiles, dark against the glaring sky. Running around the top of each ridge like a spiky coronet is an escarpment. The land is so barren and the soil so thin that the sparsely dotted trees running along the ridge tops look like a weird Mohawk hairstyle.

The Native American connection is inescapable. In all this dust and sand, surrounded by buffalo plains, monumental rocks and cliffs, it would be hard not to be reminded of an old Hollywood western. I almost expect to see smoke signals rising from behind the high ridges or John Wayne riding through the pass. I give myself a mental shake: I seem to have stepped into the wrong genre, the wrong nation.

What disconcerts me most of all, however, is that although I feel lost, I also recognise the landscape with its river red gums, its Livistona palms and bottle trees, high rocky escarpments and big, big skies—I am in a place at once familiar and unfamiliar. I have been here so many times before and yet I have never been here in my life. I cannot work out if I am in a space or a place. Slowly making a 360-degree turn, I think this location is too big to be called a place. While it has a name, as a place must, it is, in fact, one great big space. It is not empty, as most spaces are thought to be, but nor does it seem to have boundaries, as places generally have.

If my sense of space and place is confused, so is my sense of time. A few kilometres behind me is a lovely old stone homestead. Expecting to find red dirt, dust, grime and a kind of 1950s dreary dilapidation, I am surprised to find it all modern, prosperous, clean and tidy. Enclosed by an up-to-date glass veranda, the homestead is sparkling and surrounded by well-kept lawns, tall trees and flowerbeds. In the station yard are outhouses, barns, sheds, stables and workers' living quarters with far fewer old tyres and rusting farming equipment scattered around than I had imagined I would find in the outback. To my urban eyes, this station has an unusual degree of smartness and professionalism. The horses in the paddocks are all fine thoroughbreds, a well-kept crocodile farm nestles among beautifully tended, lush tropical plants, and helicopters constantly buzz in and out of the helipad. It has all the latest technology that makes home and working life comfortable, efficient, and very 21st century.

Back in the 1950s—which is when I knew it best—this station did not look particularly prosperous. The outhouses then were little more than crude shacks out of which Aboriginal workers and their families sprawled into the

Mongala Station (Coolibah Station)

yard, the women to hang up their washing, splash water from troughs on their hot, dusty bodies, and scoop up their children— piccaninnies, as the white folk called them—playing in the dust or mud. Back then, today's grassy paddocks were dry scrubland and the only communication technology consisted of a simple, shortwave pedal radio. Life then was certainly a whole lot tougher. And if there are Indigenous workers and their families living there today, I did not see them. No, it's not at all like it used to be back then. Not that I'd ever stepped foot on Australian soil the 1950s.

Inside the landscape

Let me explain. I am on Coolibah cattle station by the Victoria River in Australia's Northern Territory. It is a seven-hour drive south from Darwin, just over 200 kilometres west of Katherine and about 300 kilometres east from Kununurra. This station takes up not only geographical space; it also has a place in Australian cinematic history. This is why I know it so well. In Charles Chauvel's 1955 film *Jedda* it is called 'Mongala'. I recognise this landscape because I have seen the film so many times. I am standing in this landscape because I am writing this book about a film that bewitches me as much as it bewilders me. This sense of bewilderment seeped into my research, which involved visiting the film's locations.

Like most of Chauvel's films, *Jedda* is remarkable for the spectacular landscapes that fill the frames. They tell of the filmmaker's love for the land. Entering the actual landscape myself, rather than looking at it, I got lost. In a film the camera shows a landscape by carefully framing it through a lens, usually ensuring that the land is tastefully composed. As spectators, we look at this landscape and more often than not we see it (if we notice it at all) simply as background, the setting for the narrative and the action. In most films, especially mainstream or Hollywood, the story is so strong or the action so visually compelling that the last thing we want to do is to stop and look at the landscape.

Being physically in one of *Jedda*'s locations meant there was no narrative compelling me to draw my eyes away from the landscape. I was no longer looking at a landscape, I was inside the landscape. I was not constrained by the scriptwriters' storyline, the cinematographer's framing, or the sequence of images decided upon by the editor. I could now turn round and look back at what the film's landscape was looking at. I could see what the audience sees only if the filmmaker decides to film a shot from the point of view of the land. This does not happen often in mainstream cinema since the filmic landscape is generally only there to provide a space in which the story can unfold and the characters can fill.

In *Jedda's* footsteps

For almost two weeks, tracing the footsteps of *Jedda*'s cast and crew, I drove to the main locations in the Northern Territory where *Jedda* was filmed.[1] Coolibah Station is where, after her mother died in childbirth, an Indigenous baby (Margaret Dingle) was handed over to Sarah McMann (Betty Suttor), the white missus who unofficially adopted her, tried to 'civilise' her and brought her up as her daughter. This is where Sarah's Indigenous domestic workers, called 'lubras' in the film, named the baby 'Jedda', meaning 'little wild goose'.[2]

I paddled in the Victoria River where the teenage Jedda (Rosalie 'Ngarla' Kunoth) was wooed by the 'half-caste' Joe (Paul Reynall).[3] I wandered around the outhouses where Joe, who also grew up at Mongala station, lurked as a young boy (Willie Farrar) before growing up to be the head stockman for station owner Doug McMann (George Simpson-Lyttle). I walked where Jedda had walked under the high escarpments and along the riverbanks. I found the very the place where she first set eyes on the handsome, dark-skinned Marbuk (Robert Tudawali), a 'full-blood outlaw from the Tiwi tribe'.

Approximately halfway between Darwin and Kakadu is the Mary River at Marrakai, an area with saltwater crocodiles, freshwater billabongs, floodplains, woodlands, and paperbark and monsoon forests. This where the film's buffalo muster took place and where Jedda was abducted by Marbuk. At Nitmiluk, or Katherine Gorge as the tourist brochures still call it, I sat in the prow of a tourist boat and sped through the waters Jedda and Marbuk rafted down in an attempt to throw their pursuers off the scent. Not far south from Katherine, close to the lovely small town of Mataranka on the Stuart Highway, I swam in the idyllic water-lily pools near the

Roper River where two vicious crocodile fights were filmed. The crew also travelled along the Katherine River through Maranboy and Beswick to Mineroo in Arnhem Land where, according to the film's publicity pamphlet, 'Chauvel got some of the best scenes of wild aborigines in their natural state.'

My route took me a day's journey further south via Tennant Creek to Alice Springs. This was followed by another half-day of driving along Namatjira Drive, a beautiful road running along the base of the caterpillar-like West Macdonnell Ranges of Central Australia. Here, I walked through the spectacular Standley Chasm and waited for the midday sun to light up the dark canyon just as it had for Marbuk as he dragged the exhausted and scared Jedda after him. I clambered up rocks, wriggled through overhanging caves, and dipped my toes in the icy pool at Ormiston Gorge where Marbuk speared a fish and broke the unbreakable law of his tribal people. Under the hot early summer sun, I tramped through some of the harsh territory to which Marbuk fled with Jedda, the girl he had abducted, after his own people condemned him to death, chased by the ever-persistent Joe.

One night, while staying at Glen Helen on the banks of the Finke River, looking at *Jedda* yet again, I saw a shot I had never noticed before. Jedda and Marbuk, running from Joe and the police, are on a rocky plain, and in the background is Mount Sonder. This is a mountain made famous by the celebrated Indigenous artist Albert Namatjira, whose exquisite watercolours of desert landscapes pervade the tones of *Jedda*'s landscapes.[4]

The next day, armed with a rough map (kindly drawn by the motel manager) and my portable DVD-player, I trekked for a couple of hours through the desert and, matching the landscape in the film to the one before my eyes, I found that exact spot.

Had I not done this, I might never have found the link that screenwriters Charles and Elsa Chauvel, had forged between Marbuk and Namatjira. The artist and the film's character were both found guilty of violating the law of their people by marrying (in Namatjira's case) or consorting with (in Marbuk's case) a woman from outside their tribal classificatory kinship system. With a great deal of filmic licence, Namatjira's ostracism was turned into the death penalty for Marbuk, whose tribal elders sang him to death.

I found the terrain tough going. How much tougher, I realised, must it have been for the crew and cast with all their heavy equipment and constant worries about the fading light? I sat and thought long and hard about the shy, 16-year-old Rosalie Kunoth, who was not at all worldly. She was born in a creek bed at Utopia Station, in the Central Australian desert, the daughter of a traditional tribal woman and a father of mixed heritage or, in her own words, 'three quarters German'. For the first few years of her life she had lived with her mother's people; when she was about ten, she went to board at St Mary's convent school in Alice Springs. Rosalie would later tell television interviewer Andrew Denton that her response to feeling scared and reluctant to perform actions that went against her instincts and cultural beliefs was to sulk. To my mind, she looks more petrified than sulky in the film.

My final location—and that of the film—was in New South Wales. The dramatic and spectacular deaths of Marbuk and Jedda were filmed at Kanangra Walls, an astonishingly beautiful location in the Blue Mountains to the west of Sydney in New South Wales.[5]

So here I stood, close to the cliff edge where, by painting the orange–grey sandstone rocks red, Chauvel had contrived to

At Kanangra Falls.

match the original Northern Territory landscape. This was where Marbuk, insane by now, had plunged more than 100 metres to his death, pulling Jedda with him.

Feeling scared

It was scary standing on so high a cliff edge, Kanangra Creek barely discernible far below. Images of the last seconds of Jedda's life were replaying on the back of my retinas and echoes of her desperate scream were sounding in my ears. How much more frightening must it have been for the young convent girl acting the part? Rosalie Kunoth-Monks later said she found it difficult to communicate with Elsa Chauvel, the person who mainly looked after and coached her. There was much she did not understand about starring in a film, as she told Denton:

> I do not think I had a concept at all, no idea of what movies were about. I still have moments of anxiety when I think about it … I was nervous in that I was out of my environment, just getting used to a different language, which is English, and then being removed from that and then getting to all these crazy white fellas over there. And meeting for the first time Bob Tudawali who was scary (to me he looked scary): he was darker than my little reddish brown men from central Australia and meeting for the first time people who had a different language.

Asked by Denton about how closely she'd had to work with Tudawali, Rosalie replied: 'It took a long time for me to allow him even to touch me, 'cos that wasn't my upbringing. Nobody was allowed to touch me, you know? Especially when he had to put his arm around my waist or something …'

Unlike Jedda, Rosalie Kunoth-Monks is a survivor.[6] She was hurt by her experience but not terminally damaged. Nevertheless, I can't help but worry about how hard the experience of filmmaking must have been for her, culturally and emotionally as well as physically.

There are photos of the famous last scene being filmed. Jedda lies slumped in Marbuk's arms at the very edge of the cliff. There are ropes attached to the camera, presumably to make sure it didn't fall off the cliff. I can see no ropes attached to Rosalie Kunoth or Robert Tudawali. Is the fear on her face acting, or is it real? I suspect Rosalie was terrified. Here she is, much of her upper body exposed by her torn and tattered costume, held tightly by Tudawali, who is wearing nothing but his loincloth. She was only 15, for goodness sake. And what if she had a fear of heights and suffered from vertigo? Did anyone even ask her? There in the actual location, I felt myself empathising more deeply with the actors than I had when looking at them flickering past my eyes at 24 frames per second.

Being in this landscape also made me think more deeply about the film's ending. Australia's first-ever, Indigenous actors in main roles are both killed off. They don't even get the last word. What is this supposed to mean? Peering down at the Creek, I concluded that there could be no happy ending in a film that maps the involuntary double dislocation of an Indigenous child, first by adoption and then by abduction.

Owning and belonging

Overlooking Coolibah Station there is a spectacular high ridge, one we often see in the first half of the film as Doug and Sarah

McMann and the Aboriginal workers go about their business. The local people today call this 'Jedda's Leap' apparently unaware that Jedda never leapt there. There is another 'Jedda's Leap' at Katherine Gorge which is, it's said, where the film's ending was originally filmed. The Northern Territory seems to want to claim *Jedda* just as the film itself claims the Northern Territory.

Standing several thousand kilometres away from the Northern Territory on this cliff edge in New South Wales, helped me realise that although *Jedda* is ostensibly a Northern Territory story, it is a film whose story and locations do not belong to any one place. In short, the film and its locations have very leaky borders.

My research journey confirmed for me that the way we think of 'landscape' implies a framing of the land, which in turn, implies that a landscape is shaped by how we look at it. A frame turns land into a constructed landscape; it turns nature into culture, in other words.

If the landscape I stood in was liberated from the filmed and framed landscape of the film, then so, too, was I. Through not just looking at the landscape, but actually being *in* it, my view of the film was unframed. I was in two places at once, actual and filmic. I was also in more than one time zone. There was the here and now of 2011, the mid-1950s when the film was made, and the landscape's time, a time infinitely more ancient and with much older narratives.

Standing outside the relentless imperative of the film's narrative meant I could find the space in which to turn landscape back to land. In doing so, I caught other narratives in my sights. The issue of ownership was one such narrative. Anyone can 'own' a landscape just by looking at it, but the land itself has far older and deeper stories to tell about possession. In the history of the land we call Australia, who owned the land, and when and how ownership was manifested, has been of supreme importance ever since European settlement began in 1788, and *terra nullius*—meaning 'land belonging to no one' or 'no man's land'—was declared.

Does all—or any—of this geography matter? I think it does because of the way *Jedda* both shows and hides the implications of identity and belonging, and in the way its story and locations intertwine. There are mysteries that the narrative hints at, and yet more mysteries that the landscape suggests. Because a film is always about so much more than just its narrative, I want to share some of the mysteries I found in this film and my attempts to solve them.

Visiting the film's locations helped me see more clearly what it has to say about territory and ownership, about who belongs in what space, who is put in their place, and who is displaced and replaced. All of this has enormous implications (not only for the film's characters but also for the people represented by the fictional characters—the Indigenous peoples of the Northern Territory): by locating themselves on land already owned by others, white settlers imposed dislocation and relocation upon the land's traditional owners.

Jedda abducted by the 'primitive' Marbuk.

I
WHY *JEDDA*?

A filmic earworm

The authors of this series are asked to choose a film they feel passionate about. They do not have to *like* the film, however. The series seeks passion. I am not going to claim that I passionately dislike Charles Chauvel's *Jedda*, but I do want to make it clear from the start that I do not *love* it.

Nor am I going to claim that it is brilliantly made. The story of a black baby who is adopted by a white woman in the Northern Territory's outback, and who grows up expecting to marry a mixed-race stockman only to be abducted by the bad, mad and 'primitive' Marbuk who lures her to her death, delivers a bastardised melodrama. Technologically, there is some clunky editing and the 'day for night' technique, which is supposed to make sunlight look like moonlight, largely fails to convince. The acting from both the white professionals and the Indigenous amateurs is frequently wooden, and much of the dialogue sounds as if it escaped from a Year 7 textbook on race relations. For now, I'll say no more about the film's politics other than that when I first saw it, I thought I had never before in my life seen a film quite as racist.

For any reader who is put off by my initial reaction, I also want to say that *Jedda* is infinitely more fascinating than I first realised. There are film classics that are overtly and irretrievably racist—Leni Riefenstahl's Nazi-sponsored documentaries, *Triumph of the Will* and *Olympia*, D.W. Griffith's *Birth of a Nation* and Phil Walsh's *Birth of White Australia*, for example. *Jedda*'s treatment of race is not like these.

Perhaps the best way of describing the hold this film has over me is to say that it is the filmic equivalent of a musical earworm burrowing in my head—I cannot stop viewing and re-viewing it, nor can I work out if that is because it is attached to me, or I am attached to it. Either way, my passion for *Jedda* is not a passionate hatred. Partly, my fascination lies in how it constantly changes: I have seen *Jedda* more times than I can recall and it is never the same movie twice. I constantly watch it because I want to discover what more it has to show and tell me. It never fails me in this.

For the intense two-week period when I visited the main locations in the Northern Territory, I saw the film each night after I had visited the film's landscapes. I thought this would be hard to do. Each time I put the DVD on my laptop player in one or other motel or campsite (and once in the middle of the desert) as I travelled south from Darwin to central Australia, I thought the next 90 minutes would stretch halfway to eternity and back. Within the very first few seconds I was always sucked back in: that filmic mindworm starts burrowing in my head again and refuses to let me go.

A classic

I have no doubts whatsoever about *Jedda*'s status as a classic. There are many reasons why a film gets called a classic. For some, the term means a Hollywood movie made in the 1930s and '40s, in the heyday of the studio system. This explains why, for many Australian critics and audiences, an Australian classic is a film that successfully mimics a classic Hollywood movie. For contrarians, of course, a classic Aussie film is one that is decidedly *un*like a Hollywood movie. Aussie films tend to get damned for copying Hollywood styles and genres and, at the same time, damned for failing to live up to Hollywood's high standard of professionalism—the latter often being the result of enormous budgets.[7] Another definition of a classic film is one that has received wide critical acclaim—whether or not it earned much, or any, popular acclaim. Alternatively, it might be one that adheres to certain standards, embodies widely accepted qualities of high art, or has a long-established reputation for excellence or controversy.

Where does *Jedda* fit in these criteria? The film's relationship to Hollywood is complex: it takes a popular genre of the period, melodrama, to a completely new place, and it is hard to say whether it is too Hollywood or not Hollywood enough. Perhaps the film is telling us that this distinction is pointless. It gained a fair amount of popular and critical acclaim (probably more of the former than the latter) when it was released, but its critical success has not endured. It has certainly created a lot of controversy. I have heard of screenings at which Indigenous people walked out, leaving many white audiences staying put, uncomfortably determined to learn about 1950s race politics. And I have been at a screening where white people protested the depiction of Indigenous people while the Indigenous audiences stayed because they loved it.

So yes, *Jedda* is an Australian classic for a number of reasons. It is the first Australian-made film to have Indigenous characters

Nitmiluk, or Katherine Gorge.

at the centre of the narrative and, importantly, to cast Indigenous actors in these roles rather than have white actors in blackface, as many Australian films before and since have done. It is the first Australian-made film to be shot in colour and the first Australian film to be invited to the prestigious Cannes Film Festival.[8] As the National Film and Sound Archive website tells us, *Jedda* is historic (historic in the sense of being historically important) 'because it is arguably the first Australian film to take the emotional lives of Aboriginal people seriously'.[9] But *Jedda* is also much more than all this.

Most attempts to construct a list of criteria for a classic are flawed because fundamentally, all criticism is a matter of personal taste—and, often, prejudice. What makes *Jedda* a classic for me has a lot to do with how its meaning is not fixed. This intrigues me. I find little mysteries embedded in its story, soundtrack and images that make me want to see the film again. And again. What intrigues me most of all is the way the land is filmed and framed. I am seduced by this film, at least partly because it is so much about a land that is so obviously loved by its filmmaker.

Locationism

It is impossible to ignore the land in *Jedda*. Chauvel makes it possible for us to see his ideas about nature, culture and civilisation by the way in which he films the land. The film shows nature in terms of the land and the native people being indivisible parts of each other. This is true not only of *Jedda*, but of all his films. It is impossible to avoid seeing Chauvel's love of the Australian land in every film that he made.

His very first film, a silent western of sorts entitled *The Moth of Moonbi* (1926), led the way for all his future films. It tells of a young country girl who is attracted by the big, bad city, but who eventually learns that she belongs on the land, as a good girl should. At a time when most feature films were filmed in studios, especially a melodrama like this, Chauvel's daughter, Susanne Chauvel Carlsson, tells us:

> Three main location camps were set up – near Spicer's Peak at Franklyn Vale cattle station and under the Sleeping Assyrian, a mountain in the Rosevale Valley. The little film unit … struggled up Spicer's Gap, one of the highest point in Queensland, with tents, provisions and film equipment carried by packhorses, on a trail which was notoriously inaccessible …
> This seemed to set the pattern of all the arduous film safaris to follow.

Indeed it did. Without exception, all Chauvel's films involved location shoots, often in very rugged country, and the landscape and would repeatedly play a leading role. Coining the word 'locationism', Stuart Cunningham, one of Australia's foremost film academics and author of *Featuring Australia: The Cinema of Charles Chauvel*, describes Chauvel's films as a mixture of documentary, or social realism, resulting from 'his passion for, indeed obsession with, *location* shooting'. Cunningham admits that 'locationism' 'is an ugly word, but I can think of no better one to catch Chauvel's intense commitment – despite the massive technical and financial obstacles – to shooting the "true" country'. He's right: 'locationism' is the perfect word for it.

Reality, authenticity

'Location', in the filmmaker's lexicon, refers to the place where you set up your camera; specifically, a place outside the studio. Going 'on location' involves expense (all those people travelling to, being accommodated and fed in, places often a long way from home base) and time, always an expensive item in a filmmaker's budget. How much easier, cheaper—and often just as convincing—to shoot a film in the city studios. Or *almost* as convincing. 'Location' also refers to the place where the film story is set. This can be an imagined place but when it's an actual place, it give a sense of reality to a fictional story and helps audiences suspend their disbelief.

Few cinema publicists can resist telling audiences when a film has been shot on location, and the more exotic or foreign, the better. Authentic landscapes don't come cheap, but they are widely judged by film producers to be worth the expense. Seeing a real place and an actual landscape on the screen adds the spice of authenticity and a sense of being valued. After all, if the producers thought it worth spending so much money on actual locations, they presumably think that we, the audience, are worth it. When a filmmaker wants to create a strong impression of reality and authenticity, landscape—the sort of landscape you can only get by being on location—is invaluable. As a poster for *Jedda* boasted, 'If you took a £500 tour of Australia, you couldn't see such wondrous scenes of rugged magnificence as *Jedda* shows.'

Australia the star

Chauvel's locationism meant that he filmed not only outside the studio, but also outdoors and, often, outback. He was no stranger to the land, having been brought up in the tradition of the landed gentry in the Northern Rivers district of New South Wales and south-eastern Queensland. By first studying art, then acting and finally becoming a filmmaker, he disappointed his father, who had groomed him for life on the land. But Charles never lost his love for the soil or his support for the core national values of the land-owning class. All his films, especially *Sons of Matthew*, *Jedda* and the 13-part television travelogue series, *Australian Walkabout*, make this clear.

His daughter Susanne thought her father's taste for filming in outdoor locations was

> an extension of his boyhood fantasies, when he read every available travel or adventure book, itched to see what lay beyond the mountains encircling his valley and watched the lantern slides shown him by a German settler who had hunted big game in Africa.

She thought the Australian actor Chips Rafferty, who appeared in several of Chauvel's films, put it more bluntly: 'He's a bloody frustrated explorer.'

Looking at *Jedda* I can think only that Chauvel wanted to cast Australia at the centre of his film. As Cunningham writes, 'the concept of locationism engages with Chauvel's nationalist desire to make Australia a film star.' Landscape in *Jedda* is both the location and the setting; it serves aesthetic and narrative purposes and sometimes threatens to overwhelm the story. *Jedda* is very much about place—not just places themselves, but also about who is placed, displaced and replaced where and by whom.

Location raises issues of dislocation and relocation that lay at the heart of discussions about Indigenous peoples in white Australia in the 1950s. It still does today.

A place to start

Chauvel's locationism, the settings for the film's narrative, and the beauty of the carefully framed images of the Northern Territory landscape fascinate me. As does the idea that by showing so much actual landscape, rather than show reality, the film tries to hide it—and I think it almost succeeds. It is this tension that makes a film interesting for me: for a film to be a classic, there has to be something more to it, or about it, than how the images and sounds tell the story. A film that does not make its audiences look under the surface of its celluloid skin is probably not going to be considered a classic by very many critics or audiences. One of the essential ingredients of a classic is its ability to make audiences in each subsequent generation stop, admire and find relevance. *Jedda* has this ability.

I had been trying to write about this film ever since I first saw it, which was within a month of arriving to live in Australia in the early 1990s. I had always found an excuse not to, but was never able to identify why. I once showed a version of what I had written to a good friend and she helped me realise that it was not ready, that something was missing. Looking for something that is not there is difficult. But she was right: I did not know where to start, I did not have a beginning. I kept returning to Stuart Cunningham's book to see if it could enlighten me. Eventually, his word 'locationism' enabled me to see what was missing. It helped me understand that if Chauvel had to go to the actual locations to frame his narrative, then so did I. It was the only way I could find both his *Jedda* and mine.

II
MEETING *JEDDA*

My *Jedda*

Most of the authors in this series begin by sharing with the reader the context in which they first saw the film they chose to write about. They seem to feel compelled to describe where, why, when and how they first saw it. It's as if they need to locate themselves outside the film before they can step inside its frames to explore what they saw and heard. Now that I am writing for the series, I understand this compulsion better. It allows an author to write about *their* film. I want readers to understand that the *Jedda* I am writing about is *my Jedda*.

The more I explored the film's story in terms of its geographical coordinates, the more I found myself enmeshed in its cultural coordinates. These led me to look for—and eventually find—ideas which lay buried deep in the film's story. That these ideas were largely about displacement and replacement, dislocation and relocation, did not really surprise me. After all, one of the things that makes such an important part of Australia's cinematic heritage is that its two main characters are Aboriginal—they are even given precedence over the white actors in the credits, which could well be a world first. My point is that few real stories about Australia's first people can avoid the actuality of the stolen generations, and *Jedda* has a special connection to this aspect of the real Indigenous story.

But I am running ahead of myself. For now, I want to share how I met *Jedda* for the first time.

First encounter

As already mentioned, my first encounter with *Jedda* was not promising. The context in which I saw it is important to my story because it helped me realise that each individual member of the audience gets a sense of owning the films they see. It also made me think more deeply about how we categorise films in terms of genre and nation—where films and their filmmakers belong, in other words.

Marbuk in the west Macdonnell Ranges.

It was 1995 and I had just joined the Australian Film, Television and Radio School as the Head of Film Studies. I was keen to increase my students' knowledge of Australian national cinema and, as a recent migrant from England, my own knowledge most definitely needed improving. So I determined to include as many Australian films as I could in the courses I taught.

The first course I designed owed much to one I had recently taught in England—on the effects of colonial oppression. The films for this course included classics such as Zoltan Korda's hymn to British colonialism in Africa, *Sanders of the River*; Gillo Pontecorvo's powerful critique of French imperialism, *The Battle of Algiers*; and George Stevens' Hollywood version of Rudyard Kipling's poem about a native Indian under British rule, *Gunga Din*.

Finding myself in white settler, post-colonial Australia—the place I now call home—I adapted this course to emphasise Pacific-rim nation cinemas. The films I added for my Australian students included Jean-Jaques Annaud's *The Lover*, set in French colonial Vietnam; the Sri Lankan-born Laleen Jayamanne's *A Song of Ceylon*, which interrogates Basil Wright's 1934 British avant-garde documentary, *Song of Ceylon* (the latter commissioned by the Ceylon Tea Propaganda Board); and *Jedda*.

Jedda was the one film I had not yet seen. I was aware that it might be controversial after discovering in the School library a promotional booklet written by Charles Chauvel describing Rosalie Kunoth as 'Eve in ebony' and Robert Tudawali as a 'civilised savage.' The statement that 'Australian aborigines, like most simple native tribes, have a very deep-seated belief in, and fear of, sorcery' didn't reassure me either. While the film sounded as if it was going to fit the objectives of the course perfectly, I felt uneasy about screening this film to Australia's future filmmakers in this context. It looked very much as if I would appear to be attacking one of Australia's national treasures.

Hide and seek

I felt I first had to work out how much of *Jedda* was fact and how much was fiction. This was no easy task. While the opening credits tell us the screenplay was written by Charles and Elsa Chauvel—indicating, presumably, that it was a fictional story—the filmmakers were at pains to explain to audiences its factual basis.

With several misspellings, the first caption informs us:

> To cast this picture the producer went to the primitive Aboriginee race of Australia and now introduces NARLA KUNOTH as Jedda, a girl of the Arunta tribe and ROBERT TUDEWALLI, a man of the Tiwi tribe as Marbuk. In this film many people of the Northern Territory of Australia are reliving their roles. The story of Jedda is founded on fact.[10]

So is *Jedda* fact or fiction? Chauvel, I learned, is well known for his 'quasi-documentary' approach to filmmaking and for using actuality footage in his feature films. Chauvel himself emphasised the authenticity of the narrative, maintaining that he and his wife had found the stories while doing locational research in the Northern Territory. As he describes it in Elsa's book, *My Life with Charles Chauvel*, around the campfire each night they heard many local stories and they chose three as the basis for the narrative:

> The first of these was a tragic, but not uncommon, incident where a young mother, alone on an isolated cattle property, sought, by pedal radio, a permit to bury her dead baby.
>
> The second was the amazing story of an Aboriginal girl who was brought up by a white family in a town and educated at a private school. On a trip to the Centre, she went off with an Aboriginal tribe and refused to come back.
>
> The final in the trilogy was that of the able killer, Nemarluk. Ruthless and cunning, he was responsible for a number of murders and specialised in the abduction of attractive black women from station properties, often leaving these girls to die in the bush.
>
> These stories were adapted and interwoven to create the dramatic saga of Jedda, a girl of the Arunta tribe, who is caught up between white conventions and her sense of tribal identity.

I supposed these stories could all be true, but to my mind there was more than a touch of fantasy to them. A fantasy element seems to have started some years earlier in the USA where the Chauvels were exploring what made Hollywood so successful. Elsa tells that a *Time* magazine journalist first sowed the seeds for *Jedda* by urging Chauvel to make a film about 'those Stone Age people of yours' as this would attract overseas audiences by offering unique and exotic images of 'something that (Hollywood) cannot get the ingredients for outside your country'. Untroubled by this description of First Nation people, Elsa continues, 'The idea of the Northern Territory and its Stone Age men was always playing hide and seek enticingly in Charles's mind.'

My students, were divided like most Australians are when the first see *Jedda*. But they taught me a valuable lesson. After hearing my post-colonial critique and semi-apology for screening the film, an Indigenous student gently told me that his Aunty thought Marbuk was a bit of a spunk. This was when I realised there was much more to the film than I had credited it with. I also realised that my students, their relatives and I all owned a different *Jedda*.

This, then, is the story of how I first encountered what would become my *Jedda*. Next, I need to explore the film's story in more detail if readers who have not yet seen the film are going to make sense of my first negative reaction. Before I do, however, I have to admit that I am much more interested in what the film does not show or tell, and in what it tries but ultimately fails to hide, than in what the narrative explicitly tells us. All films are about more than their narrative, of course, and many films are less about telling than showing, more about spectacle than narrative.

Jedda combines showing and telling in a way that captures my imagination more than it captures my desire for story. It's the 'hide and seek' elements of *Jedda*'s story that intrigue me most and which I explore next.

III
JEDDA'S STORY PART I

Melodrama

Jedda's story falls into two parts, each framed by different genres. One of the main characteristics of genre cinema is that, by using a set of conventions that have become familiar to the audience, it sets up certain expectations. Audiences tend to feel satisfied when their expectations are realised, discomforted when a film appears to promise one thing but delivers another.[11] *Jedda,* it's fair to say, falls into the latter category: curiously, just when you think you know where the story is going, it veers off in another direction. As genre is important for my understanding of the film, in this and the next chapter, I focus on how *Jedda*'s story unfolds within the codes and conventions of the more obvious film genres it uses. Other, less obvious, genres lurk in the narrative, and these I explore later. This is just one of the many puzzling aspects of the film.

Jedda is often described as a melodrama, a genre of heightened emotions that attempts to make sense of the family, but you wouldn't know this from its opening sequence. It starts with a montage sequence of outback landscapes. We see aerial shots of beautiful, wide vistas of buffalo plains, river estuaries and the desert, with Uluru glowing blood red almost as vividly as it does in reality. (With a sinking heart I realise I am going to run out of superlatives to describe the landscapes in this film.)

In a voice-over narration, we hear an upper middle-class English accent. This is Joe (Paul Reynall) who most surprisingly, given his accent, introduces himself as 'the half-caste son of an Afghan teamster and an Australian Aborigine woman'. The land we are looking at, he tells us, is 'my land and the land of Jedda, the girl I loved'. Immediately, here is another puzzle: what are we to make of the past tense of 'loved'? Does it mean there is no more love? Or does it mean no more Jedda? This sets a high melodramatic tone right at the start. It will climb higher.

The next scene is unutterably sad. Sarah McMann, wife of the station owner, sits alone at a pedal radio on lonely Mongala cattle station. Her voice and body language speak of the very depths of grief. Crackling over the airwaves, a concerned male voice asks after her new baby's health and if her husband is with her. Bleakly, Sarah intones 'Just send me the certificate. You see I have to bury my baby. Doug is not here. He is still away. I haven't got my baby any more.'

There is an abrupt cut to the bright light of the outback. As it happens, on that very day an Aboriginal woman working as a cook on a nearby cattle muster dies in childbirth. 'Poor old Booloo,' says white boss drover Felix Romeo (Wason Byers) of the man who has just buried the mother of his child. 'He was very fond of that little woman of his.' Booloo, an uncredited actor, is not given the chance to become fond of his newborn baby because Romeo decides to take it to Mongala. Any qualms viewers might have concerning the propriety—or legality—of giving someone else's child away are dismissed by Romeo, who says, 'You know … Mrs McMann is one woman who *understands* these people.'

Like almost all the characters in *Jedda*, 'these people' are all played by 'real' people. 'In all,' Elsa Chauvel later wrote, 'there were only three professional artists in the cast with most of the others being "naturals" co-opted from the Territory.' Casting Wason Byers to play a drover is an example of how Chauvel used his actors to blend fact with fiction, if not always seamlessly. In real life Byers was a part owner of Coolibah Station.[12] According to the film's publicity booklet, 'His appearance gives the film added authenticity.' Perhaps. It did not, however, add anything in the way of acting skills.

The next day, Romeo and Booloo, with his baby tucked under his arm, ride into Mongala Station. Felix hears the Indigenous women sobbing loudly, and learns that they are grieving the death of Sarah's baby. 'That's bad,' Felix says. 'Maybe I'd better not see her, then.' The response from a male Aboriginal station worker is lovely: 'I think more better you do see her.' More better, indeed.

Another piccaninny

Frozen with grief, Sarah's initial response to the little black baby is despair. 'It *would* live' she says. She nevertheless agrees to take it, saying she will give it to one of the Aboriginal women on the station to look after. Interestingly, she adds, 'Doug will be glad to add another piccaninny to the tribe. He says we haven't enough for the future.' It is the first sign of the lessons in racial politics to come.

Inside the homestead—which looks like, and indeed is, a set—young Indigenous women are enchanted by the baby. In mock pidgin English one remarks, 'Funny, eh? White baby fly out; black baby fly in.' They name her Jedda, meaning 'little wild goose'. Their accent, like Joe's, is bizarre: they sound like West Indians or South Africans. The puzzles are building.

Initially reluctant to have anything to do with the baby, at one point Sarah looks at her and screams 'Take it away!' Doug's return provokes another outburst, one that is shocking in its implications. When Doug says 'Try to be brave, Sarah. There's always tomorrow. There'll always be others', she recoils and pronounces the end of their sexual relationship: 'No Doug. Never again.' Doug's clumsy attempt to cheer up his emotionally frozen wife has a certain grim charm: he suggests she get over her sorrows by taking a trip to Darwin. Sarah, however, is made of sterner stuff and will recover in her own way. She will look after the baby for a few days and, if it survives, give it to one of the nursing Aboriginal women to look after.[13]

From this atmosphere of repressed sexuality, there is a slow dissolve to a lovely sequence of cute-as-a-button baby Jedda crawling about the floor and getting under everyone's feet. Played by Margaret Dingle, 'an impish bundle of mischief and charm' as the film's promotional booklet accurately states, young Jedda wins not only Sarah's hearts but ours too. The shots of her splashing about in a makeshift shower and running down the veranda wearing nothing but a man's large akubra hat and a great big grin are enough to make the iciest of hearts melt. Sarah's warm laughter tells us that she has found a substitute for her own dead child. Joe's narration returns over these shots, and with gentle irony he tells us,

'No Doug. Never again.'

'Somehow, Sarah never did find a suitable foster mother among the tribe.' Never questioning how suitable she might be as a mother to this Aboriginal child, Sarah adopts Jedda.

A little tribal heart

As it tends to in melodrama, a small cloud appears on the horizon. Over shots of little Jedda, sweet and neat in her always freshly laundered and starched pink gingham dress playing with other rather wild-looking Aboriginal children in the yard, Joe painstakingly informs us of a problem:

> Sometimes, Jedda would escape the watchful eye of the missus.
> And in those few moments, [she would] try to learn from the
> native children the first lessons of their race, the lessons of
> tracks, and how to make them. Always there would be the
> restraining voice of Sarah McMann.

With the urgent voice of an anxious mum, Sarah cries to young Joe (Willie Farrar), 'Bring Jedda away from those piccaninnies. I can't keep her clean.'[14]

It sounds ominous—and it is. We have been introduced to the major theme of the film: Jedda will be torn between white civilisation and Indigenous culture. Here, as throughout the film, cleanliness and propriety stand for whiteness, while dirt and disruption stand for Aboriginality. As young Joe lifts Jedda out of the dust, Joe's older self continues, 'All the longing in her little tribal heart for the freedom of her tribal life was being denied her.'

Wild magpie or tame canary?

The next two scenes might well be called 'a lesson in 1950s racial politics'. It is the scene that almost startled me out of my chair when I first saw it, so overt is Sarah and Doug's racism.

Making animal tracks in the dough.

In the kitchen Sarah is baking and teaching Jedda to spell. '"F" for Froggy, "G" is for Goldfish,' she says briskly as she wields her rolling pin on a lump of dough. Jedda will have none of it. The little girl climbs over the tabletop towards the dough and, to Sarah's utter consternation, sticks her fingers in the dough to make animal tracks. She plonks Jedda back in her seat and resolutely rolls away the animal tracks. Joe's voice-over explains that the 'dark' in Jedda means white civilisation can never successfully be implanted in an essentially primitive people: 'It was a hard job trying to teach Jedda the ABC of the white child and to capture a mind constantly out in the world of her dark people.' It does not stop Jedda, however, from learning a Christian hymn. Labouring the point, Joe continues, 'Jedda had never learned the language of her tribe. Or to chant the Pintari hymnal ...' At which point little Jedda, her eyes closed tight, her hands together in prayer fills the frame as she warbles 'Little baby Jesus ...' It is not hard to get the message: this adoption story is going to end in tears.

The scene segues to Doug returning from a buffalo muster after several days, perhaps weeks. (Sarah merely holds out her hand in welcome: this is about as close they ever get now she has said 'Never again.') Shooing little Jedda out of the way, Sarah solicitously cleans up an infected cut on Doug's hand. Sarah's obsession with cleanliness could not be emphasised more clearly.

'Still trying to tame that wild little magpie into a tame canary?' Doug asks patronisingly. The film cuts to a close-up of Jedda who, seeming to understand that something important is being said about her

Sarah cleans Doug's injured hand.

future, eavesdrops from behind a door. 'She's a member of one of the oldest races in the world,' continues Doug in a singsong 'I know best' sort of tone. 'Her roots are deep in a religion and way of living that we can never understand, or wipe away. They don't tame; only on the surface.'

Sarah cannot accept Doug's argument. 'That's the old cry, Doug,' she replies and then sarcastically quotes Doug's beliefs back at him: '"They don't tame. You can't drag them from their bark hovels. They like to sleep with their dogs and their fleas."' She admonishes Doug and all those who think like him with 'You know, I often wonder if you Territorians don't find it easier to think that way.'

She surely has a point. Or has she? This, perhaps, is a further reason why the scene still makes me feel slightly sick. By not offering an Indigenous viewpoint, it encourages us to take one side or the other. But both views are underpinned by Social Darwinist ideas that Indigenous people are a dying race and much lower on the scale of humanity than white people.

Exasperated, Doug talks to Sarah as if she were a child:

> Look at Millie out there in her new gingham dress and pink comb. Butter wouldn't melt in her mouth when she's here with you. But when they're ten miles out on walkabout that dress will be on the first rock and she'll be as naked as a witchetty grub.

Again the film cuts back to Jedda, her face now serious. She seems to realise it is not just her own future that is at stake, but the future of all Indigenous peoples. Or, rather, I realise this and am projecting it on a 3-year-old child.

Sarah sticks to her well-intentioned assimilationist views, countering: 'It takes time and patience to change them ...' But Doug will not be swayed from his separationist yet also well-intentioned views, and he cuts in, 'If you've got a thousand years to give away, you can have a try. I'm sorry, Sarah, civilisation is as you see it. These people have a different pattern, that's all. Now, take young Jedda ...' 'Oh not Jedda again,' snaps Sarah. But Doug ploughs on: 'Listen, Sarah, now that the house girls and the men are going on their walkabout, why not let young Jedda go with them?' The cut back to Jedda shows her retreating a couple of steps to make very sure she is not detected. Sounding utterly reasonable, Doug continues, 'Let her have a taste of her own tribal life. Plenty of kids her age go. She's living in a sort of no-man's land. Open the cage, Sarah. Let her go to her own people while she can.'

Is it the complexity of the argument or that the argument seems to continue without an Indigenous voice that finally defeats young Jedda who now decides to slip away from the scene entirely?

From the set of her mouth we can see just how strongly Sarah disapproves of Doug's views. This conversation is deeply threatening to her since Doug is proposing that the child who has replaced her own should be sent to a place where Sarah cannot go. Sarah will not—cannot—allow this to happen. Ever the maternal colonialist, as she continues to clean up Doug's wounded hand, she says firmly:

> No, Doug, I'm not going to let that child slip back. I've done so much with her. I'd stop them all going on these stupid walkabouts if I had my way. Each year I keep them in clean dresses. I doctor their sore eyes and give them good wholesome food. And then what happens? They go bush on this *wretched* walkabout and come back to me like bedraggled skeletons. I don't know what they do.

A sly tone creeps into Doug's voice:

> It might shock your staid little heart if you did. I'll tell you what they do, Sarah. They breathe. They live like their forefathers, regaining their tribal status and pride of race. We all have our pride, Sarah. You in your home, me in my work. And these people in that once-a-year time when they become 'big fella man'.

If Sarah's assimilationist argument is fuelled by her neurotic impulse to substitute Jedda for her own dead child, Doug's argument is fed by the economic interests of a land-owning businessman. He has no objections to his Indigenous workers going on an annual walkabout: 'Because of that,' he explains, 'they come back to us better stockman.'

Sarah persists: 'But I still think it's our duty to try and do something with them. Bring them closer to our way of living.' Sarah's desire—need—to eradicate the black from Jedda reveals itself in her turn of phrase that is inescapably Pygmalion: 'I really believe I can *make* something of Jedda.' 'Well,' responds Doug smugly, 'you won't do it by shutting her window at night to keep out the cry of the corroboree, dance and the didgeridoo. And you won't wipe out the tribal instincts and desires of a thousand years in one small life.'

Joe, the enigma

Doug has had enough. He withdraws his hand from Sarah's ministrations, picks up his akubra and goes outside. Determined to have the final word, he turns and says, 'And don't kid yourself about the duty stuff. That kid's really got into your hair. You've grown fond of her.' At which point, young Joe, who is loitering by the door, pipes up: 'I've grown fond of 'er too, Boss.' Doug softens, 'Well, the Jezebel,' he smiles. 'Not satisfied with claiming my wife, she claims my head stockman too.' Trotting after the boss, Joe asks in an inexplicable cockney accent, 'Eh, boss ... didyah mean wot yer said 'bout me bein' 'ed stockman?' 'That's right, Joe,' Doug replies kindly, 'one day you'll be head stockman.' Both Sarah and Doug, it seems, are capable of loving an Aboriginal person but not the same one. Why can't they both love Jedda and Joe?

The scene ends with the camera on young Joe as Jedda skips up to take his hand. The two children then walk off together through the yard—a piece of film language that tells us they are destined to be together always inside a genre that leads us to expect that they will be pulled apart. In addition to the strong emotions this scene leaves me with, it presents another puzzle: why do we never see young Joe, Jedda's only playmate and Coolibah's future head stockman, inside the homestead? Why is his place forever outside in the yard? Is it because he is half Indigenous?

Sarah's argument against the walkabout fails: each year she sees off the station workers, warning them to keep their piccaninnies away from the water's edge because of the crocodiles. This woman really does believe she is the source of all civilisation and knowledge. However, she gets her way with Jedda, who stays behind the picket fence and waves 'her people' goodbye. It suddenly occurs to me to ask why Doug has no plans to send Joe on a walkabout.

He is something of an enigma, is Joe.

Plans for Jedda

By the time she is 16, the tensions pulling Jedda (Rosalie Kunoth)—first towards the 'longing of her tribal heart' and then towards white 'civilisation'—loom larger. When Jedda wistfully dreams of going on a walkabout, Sarah is appalled: whatever would she do in the bush with 'all those naked monkeys'? With her hair neatly brushed and wearing a clean, demure dress, Jedda finds this funny and replies, 'Do what all those monkeys do, I suppose.' Sarah can hardly believe her ears. 'What nonsense,' she shoots back. 'You're no more like them than night is to day.' There is a total lack of irony in these words, though they are spoken by a very white-skinned woman to her very dark-skinned adopted daughter. Just as a trip to Darwin was Doug's solution for Sarah's grief upon losing her baby, so now it is Sarah's solution for Jedda's sadness at being unable to learn the language and culture of her people. Sarah explains that she has other plans for Jedda: 'I want you to go on living like a white girl. Like my own daughter.'

Sarah is not the only one with plans for Jedda. The mother-daughter heart-to-heart we have just seen is immediately mirrored by a man-to-man talk between Doug and the adult Joe

(Paul Reynall). Joe is now Doug's head stockman, and he wants to marry Jedda. Doug is delighted, not least because it will put an end to Sarah's worries—her 'one great fear has been the girl might mate with one of the tribes.' Not 'make love' or 'have children with' note, but 'mate', as in what animals and Aboriginal people do.

Meanwhile, Jedda's sore heart is not to be appeased by a shopping trip. In a moment of amazing—almost alarming— melodramatic excess, Jedda breaks down at her piano practice. Earthy, 'native' rhythms and tribal songs disrupt the classical western music she is playing. The camera zooms in on tribal war artefacts (spears and shields) hanging on the wall, their asymmetrical patterns contrasting with the straight lines formed by the piano keys. 'What's the matter?' asks Joe in an amused tone. 'The ghost of your tribe chasing you with a big stick?'

Joe is a success story for assimilation; having lost the cockney accent he had as a child, he sounds every bit the Oxbridge-educated, white English gent. Not that it does him any good. In keeping with the conventions of a melodrama, there needs to be a plot point about now to upset all these plans. I think we know that Joe is not going to win his girl. And once Marbuk enters the scene—which he is about to do—Joe does not stand a chance.

Enter Marbuk

Seeing Marbuk, an incredibly handsome, dark-skinned man (much darker than Joe), his body oiled and cicatrised with tribal initiation marks—and wearing only a scarlet loincloth—Jedda almost faints with desire.

Or, rather, this teenager, in her first and only experience as an actor, looks as if she is trying hard to show sexual desire. She does not convince. Each time I see the film, and this shot in particular, I cannot help but feel sorry for Rosalie. To my mind, the only convincing actor in the film is Robert Tudawali. As Marbuk, he not only looks magnificent—the Indigenous women at Coolibah all melt with lust the minute they set eyes in him— but he also acts magnificently. Joe might be a bit of a dunderhead, but not even he can fail to notice the sexual power that Tudawali invests in his character. Seeing Marbuk for the first time, Joe's first thought is to insist this loincloth-clad man put on trousers. Joe then looks at Jedda, notices that her mind has gone to a place of which he knows nothing, and immediately takes her away from this disturbing 'wild feller' to propose to her. Sorry, Joe. Too late.

Noticing the teenage Jedda, Marbuk asks, 'What one that?' A station worker warns, 'She not your skin; she wrong tribe for you.'[15] But this is melodrama, so we know that nothing is going to stop Marbuk from having what undoubtedly will be his very evil way with Jedda.

Jedda is aroused by the alluring man whose eyes follow her about. She needs to find out what the domestic servants are whispering about him. Emphasising just how much white 'civilisation' Sarah has drummed into her adopted daughter, Jedda bribes Nita with a sparkly bracelet, much as the white colonialists offered trinkets to the natives of the lands they invaded, to explain what it means to say, 'A feller sing a girl to him.' Barely audibly, Nita whispers, 'He take mating wompoo pigeon ... he eat 'em ... then call her to his blanket ...'

Jedda can make little sense of the Indigenous myths served up by the Chauvels.[16] And, in case the audience also finds it hard to understand, over a shot of Jedda looking confused and virginal in freshly laundered pyjamas, Joe's narration spells it out: 'Nita whispered to her the mysteries of the dark man's mating. How he could sing a girl to his campfire. Even against her will. The thought started to weave a spell upon the native mind of Jedda.'

That night, Jedda stares out through her bedroom window at the moonlight. Joe tells us she hears the sounds of her people making love by the billabong. Her face half clouded by shadow, Joe reads her thoughts for us: 'The throb of the didgeridoo. What did it mean? Something Jedda *longed* for yet couldn't quite understand.'

She soon will. But it will take a switch in genre for this to happen.

IV
JEDDA'S STORY PART 2

Travelogue

Until now, *Jedda* has been shaping up as a melodrama, a very Australian one, with a touch of the rite of passage genre thrown in for good measure. But a melodrama, nevertheless. However, the film takes a different turn not long after Marbuk arrives at Mongala. Several different generic turns, in fact.

First, picking up from the opening sequence, the film swings into travelogue mode. In this, Chauvel's quasi-documentary and 'locationist' impulse is strongly supported by the magical artistry of cinematographer Carl Keyser. Keyser's first film credit was as camera operator on *The Overlanders*. Directed by British documentary filmmaker Harry Watt, that film is about a wartime drover who takes a mob of prime beef cattle across 2600 kilometres of hazardous country from the Northern Territory to Queensland. If this sounds familiar it is doubtless because Baz Luhrmann borrowed much of its narrative for his film *Australia*. I think it's fair to say that *The Overlanders* has even more documentary realism and authenticity than *Jedda*.

As *Jedda*'s story takes us on a journey from Coolibah to the buffalo hunt, Keyser's images are superb. The red land and rusty-apricot colours of the sandstone rock formations look stunning against a bright, clear blue sky. Dust swirls under the feet of the horses as they are rounded up to the crack of whips. A small Aboriginal boy runs to jump up on the back of an open truck already loaded with the station workers and it drives on bumpily into the extraordinarily beautiful landscape. But we ain't seen nothin' yet; Keyser pulls out all the stops and lets us have it when the buffalo hunt begins.

To the sound of gunshots, thousands of frightened magpie geese take flight from an expanse of water. There are more shots and hunters on horseback, rifles cocked, thunder through wide, open terrain, swerving round the anthills and palm trees. A herd of buffalo runs this way and that as the hunters ride seriously hard after them, take aim, and shoot. The enormous, shaggy animals are stopped in their tracks, then keel over and die; hundreds of raptors circle ominously overhead. Along a river, the paperbarks bend gracefully, their branches sweeping the ground, as yet more buffalo rampage past.

At the day's end, Aboriginal children float among the pink waterlilies collecting tucker in their coolamons. Lissom young women, baskets with the day's catch up on their heads, sway seductively as they make their way back to camp, where the menfolk are drying the buffalo hides and rubbing sticks to light a fire. It has been a few powerful minutes of travelogue respite from the melodramatic excesses of the film's first half. The horses and buffalo hint of another genre altogether, but more of that later.

Singing *Jedda* to his blanket

Melodrama does not completely disappear, however. That night it returns with a vengeance, when Jedda is lured out of her tent to the sound of Marbuk singing her to his blanket. Unable to take her eyes off Marbuk's body gleaming in the moonlight, or resist the mystical sounds of chanting, clap sticks and didgeridoo, she feels compelled to dance to the native rhythms, as any 'true' Aboriginal girl should. But this she cannot do, of course. All Sarah's white 'civilising' education has not permitted her to learn her black culture. All those piano lessons made sure of that. Poor Jedda.

Just in case we've missed the auguries of madness and (black) magic, as the drama gathers momentum and the 'authentic' Indigenous music grows louder, there's a shot of dark clouds passing over the full moon. By now Jedda is bewitched and easily captured by Marbuk, who promptly sets fire to the camp and, clutching a screaming Jedda, runs off with her. Jedda might be attracted to Marbuk she hasn't asked to be abducted.

Over the extraordinarily realistic shots (and fine editing) of pandanus trees exploding in flames and horses panicking among the fire and smoke, a distraught Sarah is heard shrieking: 'Jedda! I can't find Jedda! Jedda! Jedda! Have any of you lubras seen Jedda?' But Jedda has gone and it looks like she's gone with Marbuk. Joe stoutly rebuffs Doug's greater concern for the horses than for Jedda and insists on going after her. 'That's my girl', he tells Doug and Sarah, the only parents he and Jedda have ever known, 'the girl I'm going to marry.' With a couple of station hands to help him, Joe rushes out of frame and into another genre. Doug may not be worried about Jedda but he is concerned about Joe's safety and he gives Joe a couple of young Aboriginal stockmen to join him on the search.

This is the second time Sarah loses a child. Perhaps it is all too much for her for we never see Sarah again. But right now I'm curious: why is Doug more worried about his horses and

Jedda captive.

about Joe's safety than he is about Jedda, his wife's adopted daughter who has lived with him in his homestead since she was a tiny baby?

Adventure-chase

The film now swings into an adventure-chase genre. With Jedda in his grasp, Marbuk sets off across country with Joe in hot pursuit. The almost predictable images of an adventure film come thick and fast. There are two exciting crocodile fights Marbuk wins one, the crocodile wins the other, and amid much gurgling we say goodbye to one of Joe's helpers. We watch a gut-churning scene where Marbuk forces Jedda to eat snake. And, with an accompaniment from a mystical, angelic choir, there is some spear-fishing among the coloured rocks of central Australia.

With Jedda as his prisoner, Marbuk heads down river towards his own tribe while Joe pounds along after them. They pass through the glorious locations I've already described from my own visit: huge flat plains under enormous skies; high mountain ridges with their scrubby trees; pale ghost gums stark against red rock and soaring cliffs; tree-lined rivers and palm-fringed velvet green pools scattered with water lilies. Chauvel's quasi-documentary impulse means that actuality keeps breaking through this captivity-adventure-chase narrative. Inevitably, the landscape is tamed by being framed and so appears less than authentically 'real'.

Another bit of actuality arrives in the form of Tas Fitzer in the role of a police officer. The film cuts back to Mongala, where Fitzer informs Doug that he is searching for an escaped criminal. No big surprise that this turns out to be a blackfella, by the name of Marbuk, who had been serving a life sentence for murder and 'had a habit of stealing lubras from the station blacks'. The film's publicity booklet announces that Fitzer is:

> ... one of the most colorful members of the Northern Territory Mounted Police ... In real life, Constable Fitzer roamed the terrible country of the East Kimberley for several years before eventually capturing the famous aborigine outlaw, Namarlurck [sic].

The mix of fact and fiction here also tells us something about Chauvel's concern for the realities of Indigenous life. Chauvel certainly knew about the actual Nemarluk (c.1911–40), an Aboriginal resistance fighter who repelled all who intruded upon his tribal lands—whites, Japanese and Indigenous people from other tribes. Chauvel would also have known of the book *Nemarluk: King of the Wilds* by the popular Australian writer Ion Idriess. Idriess gives a sympathetic account of Nemarluk's life, expressing respect and admiration for him and for his 'brave and murderous attempts to thwart the invasion of his lands'.[17] Though he based Marbuk on Nemarluk, Chauvel completely ignored his heroism and used only aspects of his criminality.

Imaginative geography

Before leaving Mongala with his police posse to join the hunt for Marbuk, Fitzer explains to Doug where he believes this outlaw is going: 'He'll work back around the swamps, through the red mountains, and across into the hidden city.' Revealing Marbuk's total disregard for all law, black and white, he adds, 'Of course that's taboo country, but he'll break all taboos if he knows the police are after him.'

Fitzer's sense of geography adds confusion to the landscape. None of it makes sense to anyone who knows the actual locations and where they are in relation to each other. The three parties—Marbuk and Jedda, Joe and his helpers, and the police posse led by Sergeant Fitzer—are filmed in a number of locations that make no geographical sense whatsoever. Not that this matters necessarily—filmmakers do it all the time. To use a term coined by Edward Said, *Jedda*'s cartographic license is the product of Chauvel's rich 'imaginative geography', an idea that helped me understand Chauvel's relationship to land and landscape when I was doing my own bit of locationism.[18]

According to the images on the screen, Marbuk and Jedda's journey starts at the buffalo camp at Marrakai, north-east of Katherine. Next we see them at Mataranka, a small township on the Roper River, a few kilometres southeast of Katherine. They then travel southwest to the West Macdonnell Ranges, a hike of several days. We then find them back north again in territory to the northeast of Mataranka, where they encounter Marbuk's tribe. From here they apparently float down a river that in the real world ends in the Gulf of Carpentaria in the north-east, but in the film takes them to Katherine Gorge—this would have meant, improbably, floating upstream.

Joe is filmed more or less where he should be according to the narrative—that is, not far behind the girl he loves— although at times he seems to be in the wrong river. The police, on the other hand, while supposedly closing in on their quarry, are sometimes wandering about the buffalo plains of the Victoria river and Marrakai where the abduction journey first began.

Nitmiluk, or Katherine Gorge.

There are those who think that for a filmmaker to take such liberties with geography is akin to telling a lie. Writing in 1987, Mudrooroo (Colin Johnson) argued:

> Aborigines believe proper location is important, and that a film, to be authentic, has to be made where the story came into being. This is important in pointing to an Aboriginal critical standard which states that a story or film to be Aboriginal must be 'authentic' in its depiction of characters, in its situation, and in its plot.

Mudrooroo wrote this years before Indigenous filmmakers became such a large and valued part of Australian cinema, and many contemporary Indigenous filmmakers clearly think differently. I can't say I have ever found it a problem for a film to play with geography. As I saw for my own eyes when in the film's locations, the very act of filming the land turns it into a visual artefact in much the same way that a map does. For me, neither the narrative nor the spectacle is any less valuable when treated imaginatively.

Against her will

The next scene is important for Jedda, for Rosalie Kunoth, and for my own feelings towards the film. In it, Marbuk breaks an important tribal law and so becomes a criminal in the eyes of Indigenous and non-Indigenous law. Ultimately, it will lead to Jedda's death, making her the double victim of Indigenous and non-Indigenous culture.

It starts as an exterior wide shot among the gorgeous coloured rocks at Ormiston Gorge in the West Macdonnell Ranges. Reds, pinks and greys are reflected in a pool of still water. In a long shot, Marbuk appears as a tiny figure with a tall spear, standing in the enormous mouth of a cave that is unmistakeably vulva-shaped. To the sound of heavenly choir voices, we see his small, lithe body running along a rock ledge just above the pool, then spearing a fish and diving in after it. (Now knowing just how cold this water is, I again pause at this shot and imagine what the experience of filming it can have been like. For Tudawali's sake, I fervently hope there were not too many takes.)

Marbuk climbs out of the water and starts to climb the rock layers, which look like a giant's staircase. At the top a fire is burning. The choir fades and the music track mixes to an echo-y male voice chanting in what may well be an authentic Indigenous language. From a close-up of the fish on the fire, the camera pulls back to reveal Marbuk cooking and Jedda cowering behind a rock at the back of the cave. The last time we saw Jedda half-hidden at the back of a shot, she was eavesdropping on Sarah and Doug debating about whether her future was in white 'civilised' or black 'primitive' society. Jedda did not get a vote then and she will not get one now. Marbuk is singing her to him and we know from what Nita whispered back at Mongala that Jedda will be unable to resist. In a shot that opts for excess in favour of subtlety, Marbuk looks at Jedda lasciviously while stroking a long spear in his lap.

Jedda is almost overcome by the spell Marbuk weaves. He throws some fish towards her which wakes her a little, and she slowly edges towards it, closer to the man she must, but cannot, resist. Marbuk sings on. Jedda's eyes droop, her head flops, she sways and finally falls back. The music makes a shrieking, pouncing sound to warn us of what is about to happen. It is too late to warn Jedda. Marbuk gives a sly half smile. Jedda lies before him, prone, insensible.

Marbuk sings Jedda to him.

At this point I cannot help but stand back from the narrative and think that the teenage Rosalie could have had no idea how the camera would emphasise her voluptuous breasts under a wet, and torn and clinging blouse, her bare shoulders, her badly ripped skirt.

Nothing will stop Marbuk now. He makes his move, edging close to the comatose Jedda. He puts out his hand towards her ankle ... Using a well-known filmic cliché, the film cuts abruptly to a close-up of the fire. The flames flicker. The embers glow. The music pulsates. We have seen nothing but we know exactly what has happened. Marbuk has broken his tribe's unbreakable law, as Joe euphemistically explains. Jedda is lost to white civilisation.

Over the years, some critics and audiences have passed over this scene with barely a mention. Others have discussed it in terms of Jedda's sexual desire, of the failure of white assimilation to quell Jedda's essential primitive urges, and of how Jedda allows herself to be 'sung' and is thus a willing, if passive, victim of her own lust. Some have written about Marbuk's successful seduction and even of a 'marriage' between the pair. All this misses an important point.

We know, because Joe has told us, that Marbuk practises 'the mysteries of the dark man's mating. He could sing a girl to his campfire. Even against her will.' What is not to know or understand about this? In law, any act of sexual intercourse without a person's consent, whether by physical force, coercion, abuse of authority or with someone who is incapable of valid consent, is rape. It is very clear from the images that Jedda is incapable of giving valid consent. Once she saw the completed film at its Darwin premiere Rosalie Kunoth understood the scene, as she told interviewer Andrew Denton:

… the thing that stuck with me at the end of that screening was the realisation that one of the scenes depicted Bob Tudawali grabbing me by the ankle. And I realised then, that film was meant to say that Bob had sex with me and that horrified me no end. Ours is such a strict rule that nobody, no other men supposed to be touching you intimately, like Bob had to touch me in that film. And I really was terrified of my tribal family seeing that film. So you could imagine my confusion and my hurt that I did not know what I'd got myself into.

The overwhelming landscape

The film does not linger on this scene. We are immediately plunged back to the chase, and from here on the narrative is mostly overwhelmed by the landscape. The travelogue re-emerges as Marbuk kills Moonlight (another uncredited Indigenous actor) in a hand-to-hand fight, Jedda, with her shirt ever more torn, tries to run away but is defeated by the treacherous terrain. Joe plods on after his girl, and Tas Fitzer keeps on tracking. This is all the stuff of an adventure chase movie but in *Jedda* the extraordinarily lovely landscape dominates.

Navigating down a river (I have seen the paperbark trees they used for their raft!), Marbuk and Jedda reach Marbuk's tribe. Chauvel's imaginative geography means that this river is a collage of different waterway locations. I recognise the Roper River, the waterlily pools at Mataranka and Katherine Gorge. Again, it is only confusing to those who know the actual locations; it does not spoil the narrative. In any case, the main point is spectacle, and to my eyes the film's supremely beautiful landscapes are only enhanced by its apparent variations

To yet more heavenly voices, Marbuk enters his own tribal lands and the film adds the anthropological documentary to its heady mix of genres. The men carry spears. They wear only penis sheaths and body paint. The naked-breasted women cool their babies in the river and look on as the men paddle their long canoes in the velvety green waters. It is one place in the film where the voices and accents cause no problem. We can hear male voices and it sounds as if it really could be a recording of Indigenous voices. Chauvel acknowledges the sound recordings of anthropologist A.P. Elkin in the credits and this is probably what we are hearing.

And have I mentioned that the landscape overwhelms with its coloured rocks, rugged mountains, lush palm-fringed pools and wide plains of long, native grasses and tall anthills, all of which are magnificent, glorious?

Native exotica?

The extras playing Marbuk's tribe are depicted as dignified people. We see them in their canoes and on the river bank, the men holding spears in loincloths and the women, their breasts naked, all with rather spectacular body paint designs. They are at peace with their world and angry with Marbuk and Jedda, for both are judged to have broken tribal law. Representing primitive, pre-contact tribal people, they do not look as if they are being coerced—and I very much doubt they were. Nonetheless, the scene troubles me.

On the one hand, the film suggests that these Indigenous people have true cultural autonomy. They are the people of the 'never never', perhaps. And why not? After all, this scene was filmed near Elsey Station, the home of Mrs Aeneas (Jeannie) Gunn, who wrote the celebrated pioneering classic, *We of the Never*

Never, about her experience in 1902 on an outback station not far from Mataranka. On the other hand, Chauvel's documentary impulse leaves a bitter aftertaste of the role many early 20th century anthropologist filmmakers played in bolstering white colonial rule.[19]

Have these extras, as Stuart Cunningham asks, been included as 'native exotica, displayed salaciously and naively for the voyeuristic pleasure of a 1950s white audience'? Deciding that this is an unfair judgement on Chauvel, Cunningham answers his own question: 'Only if it is affirmed at the same time that Chauvel dramatizes his understanding of the full range of black experience with a force and centrality.' I see his point but am less convinced. Each time I see these scenes I think Cunningham gives Chauvel the benefit of a doubt that I cannot quite give.

The encounter with the tribe is not a happy one for either Marbuk or Jedda. Joe's narration breaks in to remind us that Jedda is the 'wrong skin' and to tell us that, having broken an unbreakable law, Marbuk will be punished by being 'sung' to death and Jedda will be punished by the women. This seems harsh on Jedda, who has had no say in her fate, but Mudrooroo points out that in an Aboriginal reading of the film, both have broken the law, so both deserve to die.

Marbuk drags the increasingly dirty, bedraggled and tearful Jedda through a dry, barren but beautiful (of course) landscape. (It was here that I found the shot of the couple scrambling over some rocks near the Finke River with Mount Sonder in the background.) The film cuts back to Fitzer and his posse, apparently closing in on the couple, even though I now know that Jedda and Marbuk are in very different territory, almost 1000 kilometres away from where the police were filmed. The same goes for Joe who, while supposedly within cooee of his girl, is filmed in Katherine Gorge and other locations. No matter, the travelogue is back in full force and, as the landscape gets more and more powerful, Marbuk starts to lose his mind. Laughing manically, he decides that Jedda must die if he is to be saved.

One of us?

Suddenly, we are in completely different landscape. Over the rocks at Kanangra Walls in the Blue Mountains of New South Wales, which the crew painted ochre red to make them look as if the characters are still in the Northern Territory, Marbuk pulls the petrified Jedda closer and closer to the cliff edge. Fitzer and his men take aim but do not shoot: if Marbuk falls, so will Jedda. Pleading hysterically with Marbuk to let her go, Joe fails to realise that his every entreaty makes Marbuk take a step back. Marbuk falters. Over they go. In a wide shot we see them tumble down through the air several hundred metres to the creek below. Jedda's blood-curdling scream fills the air.

I have seen this scene very many times. Each time my heart misses a beat. Not simply because Jedda is dead, but also because I feel strongly that killing off the main protagonists is no way to end this film. They are, after all, not only the first leading roles for Indigenous characters but they are also played by Indigenous actors. The film seems to say that, ultimately, the land wins. And the land we see is Chauvel's framed land. What's more, Doug's cultural separatist argument also seems to win: no amount of piano lessons and clean clothes have been able to remove Jedda's essential blackness. Certainly the melodrama is too heavy for my liking. We know from the start it is going to end in tears—but did it have to be such a shocking and so very final a death? And

Filming at Kanangra Walls.

Closer to the edge.

did it have to be at the hands of a fellow Indigenous person? All of this takes even the normal excesses of melodrama too far for me. It makes me think something else is going on.

The film does not quite end here. The camera returns to the utterly distraught Joe. Head bowed, he staggers towards the camera, which tactfully tilts up and away from his grief-stricken face to the sky. Here, wild geese flap serenely by. In his clipped Oxbridge tones, which seem more out of place than ever, Joe intones:

> Was it our right to expect that Jedda, one of a race so mystic and removed, should be one of us in one short lifetime? The Pintaris whisper that the soul of Jedda now flies above the lonely plains and the mountain crags with the wild geese. And that she is happy with the great mother of the world in the dreaming time of tomorrow.

Joe's last words—the final words of the film—leave me with a puzzle that has been growing. It relates to the film's very first words, also Joe's, where he introduces himself and reveals himself as 'the half-caste son of an Afghan teamster and an Australian Aborigine woman'. What does he mean when he talks of Jedda being not 'one of us'? Who *is* Joe? To whom does he belong? Why does he talk like a white Englishman? And what genre does he belong to?

V

LOCATING JOE

Solving puzzles

To solve the puzzles scattered throughout *Jedda*—the strange accents, the confusion of genres, Joe's place in the story—I decided I would have to re-frame how I looked at film. In terms of genre, although nothing had prepared me for all the uniquely Australian landscape and Chauvel's locationism, I had been warned to expect melodrama. The film's poster says it all: it shows Jedda slumped across Marbuk's arms, with the words 'It was DEATH for him to look on this Girl!' blazoned across the top.

Even without these signs, the film's narrative excesses, the exaggerated, stereotypical characters, the persistent musical overkill and the performance style of the actors combine to deliver a melodrama recognisable from many Hollywood family melodramas of the period.[20] It is made less conventional by the travelogue and anthropological documentary style that dominate the second half but it could be said that these only reinforce the melodrama by heightening the tragedy of Jedda's abduction, the heartache of Sarah's childlessness, the hysteria of Marbuk's madness and the hopelessness of Joe's desires. Hollywood director Sidney Lumet once said, 'In a well-written drama, the story

Joe and Jedda.

comes out of the characters. The characters in a well-written melodrama come out of the story.' What distinguishes *Jedda* is that the melodrama comes out of the landscape.

Another genre

The sheer quantity of landscape images, as well as their overwhelming beauty, kept pulling me towards another genre. I have already hinted which one when I wrote about what it was like to stand in the film's landscape, and how I half-imagined that John Wayne was about to appear. *Jedda*'s connection to the western starts in its opening sequence. There is something seriously out of place in this opening title, or credit, sequence. It is unusual in that audiences do not generally anticipate it, especially not by those who have just seen the lurid posters of a tattered and torn Jedda swooning in the arms of the wild-looking, half-naked Marbuk as they entered the cinema.

The first image carries the names of cast and crew over a painting of what looks suspiciously like the mesas and valleys of the American mid-west frontier territory that we have all seen in a hundred Hollywood westerns. Next, there is a map of semi-charted territory that zooms out to reveal Australia, a land of the last frontier, the dotted state boundaries suggesting, perhaps, that borders have yet to be settled. The map is followed by a painting of what might be a burnt homestead or wooden fencing in the foreground, with more wild, untamed mesas and big, wide country in the background. The font used for the cast and crew credits, moreover, looks like it might have fallen off the back of a wagon from a Buffalo Bill movie. This is followed by the sequence I described earlier: the aerial shots of a great, untameable expanse of desert with a monumental rock. This is, in fact, Uluru, but after the preceding images it feels like a substitute for Monument Valley.

Despite the map with a kangaroo set firmly in the Northern Territory and the shot of Uluru, this sequence is so redolent of a classic Hollywood western that it is more than a little bewildering in a film widely considered to be a classic example of Australian national cinema and so frequently described as a melodrama. If the title sequence does not altogether promise what the rest of the film delivers, it nevertheless suggests that it would be worth looking more closely for links between *Jedda* and the western.

I am not the only one to think the Hollywood western has influenced *Jedda*. Leading Australian cinema analyst Tom O'Regan describes *Jedda* as a 'hybrid western melodrama' and likens it to King Vidor's *Duel in the Sun*. This is an apt comparison, because *Jedda* shares several concerns with this Hollywood movie, which is about a young woman of mixed race (father Anglo, mother Native-American) torn between a veneer of 'nice' white civilisation and her dark, sexual instincts, which ineluctably draw her towards an evil man and a gory death. A reviewer in the British political magazine *The New Statesman* wrote of Vidor's western: 'As sexual melodrama with spectacular background it is in its way remarkable.' The same is true of *Jedda*.

Knowing one's place

The western-melodrama genre seemed a good place to start looking but it did not quite solve the problem I had in trying to situate Joe. For this, I had to look someplace else. This thought helped me realise that I needed to investigate how Jedda treats the notion of 'place'. From the very start everyone wants *Jedda* to be in another place: Felix Romeo removes her from her father because he thinks she ought to be at Mongala Station; Sarah installs her as the replacement for her dead child and later suggests Jedda goes to Darwin to get over her longings to be elsewhere; Doug wants to send her away from Mongala to go a walkabout; Joe wants to place her in a little cottage as his wife; and Marbuk forces her to go to places all over the Northern Territory. Then there's Joe hanging around outside the homestead in the yard, never inside, and Sarah's obsession with tidiness and cleanliness—keeping everything in its right place. Place is a powerful metaphor in *Jedda*.[21]

Looking at *Jedda* once more, this time keeping in mind common phrases such as 'a place for everything and everything in its place', 'out of place', 'to know your place' and 'to be put in one's place' helped me to see the film in a new light. I noticed what the film had to say about what is, and is not, 'in its proper place' in 1950's society. Some things and characters are considered appropriate here but not there. It is inappropriate for young Jedda to be outside in the dirt rather than inside the homestead, but appropriate for young Joe to be outside the homestead, not in it. Just as the definition of dirt is 'misplaced matter', whatever is considered inappropriate in *Jedda* is treated as something that is 'out of place'. The idea of 'place' is further connected to taste, tradition and culture—not all nations and races, for example, agree on what should take place where. Unequal power relations are also involved: some people and not others have the right to tell people where they should be and where they cannot go.

Applying these ideas to *Jedda*, I found what I'd previously missed: the film hides, often in full sight, a belief that if the land needs to be civilised and subject to white order and re-order, then so do its traditional owners and inhabitants. How could I have missed all the ideas lurking within the film's images and words relating to issues of location, dislocation and relocation, and specifically the 'out of place'? What else is the map with its state boundaries in the title sequence but evidence of how the white settlers charted, ordered and re-ordered the land? It suddenly seemed obvious that I would have to look much more closely at what the film was saying—and not saying—about Joe's proper place on the station, in the story, and in the film frames. This, I would discover, was closely related to the genre he found himself in.

Looked at through the prism of ideas about space and place, the opening scene, where we are first introduced to Joe, tells a different story. Sitting alone, lonely and grieving, Sarah should obviously be someplace else—possibly in the nearest hospital, where her baby might have been saved. Doug is clearly not in his rightful place: he should be at his wife's side at such a time. But before this, already two things about Joe are very much out of place. In the credits, the characters' names are all listed as one would expect—Jedda, Marbuk, Sarah McMann, Douglas McMann, and so on, with the actor's names beside them. Apart, that is, from Joe. Unlike all the others, his name is placed in inverted commas and his race is given. So, we see the words: 'Joe (half caste).' Then there's the matter of his voice: what *is* an Afghan-Aboriginal man in the outback doing with an Oxbridge accent in this movie?

Another genre

Bit by bit we learn things about Joe that don't add up. He tells us he was adopted by Doug and Sarah McMann when he was a child, but not why. Nor do we learn why Doug implicitly names Joe as his heir. Doug is obviously fond of him—much more than he is of Jedda—but he does not treat Joe like a son. He is treated separately and differently from the full-blood 'piccaninnies', but still he has no place inside the homestead. To unravel Joe's mystery I needed to find out where he came from. And to do this, I first had to explore Chauvel's fascination with the western.

The western was one of Hollywood's most popular movie genres in the 1940s and 1950s, and as Chauvel was determined to make a film that would succeed critically and financially in the US, it was an obvious genre for him to use. But Joe's mixed-race heritage suggested that I should turn my attention from the western-melodrama to the Native-American sub-genre. This has a long history of reinforcing racist ideas while also questioning such ideas by including roles for 'half-castes', and casting white actors to play Indians in red-face.

Chauvel was no stranger to either the western or the Native-American sub-genre. When learning about movie-making in Hollywood in the early 1920s, he found work as an extra on several westerns due to his skill with horses and he was often cast as a Mexican or Indian, which he played in red face. Susanne Carlsson Chauvel tells that Michael Pate, an Australian actor whom Chauvel cast in several films, knew her father in Hollywood and recalled that he

> Handled himself like a true Australian bushie, in one shot galloping right-to-left as a Red Indian, the next hurtling by in the same direction, even on the same horse, as a cowboy chasing the same Red Indian (himself).

Back home in Australia, Chauvel's first two silent films used the red-face convention of the western—as did many Australian films of the period. In *Moth of Moonbi*, he cast a local white woman to play an Aboriginal woman in blackface, and in *Greenhide*, Chauvel himself put on blackface to play an Aboriginal stockman. His love for this sub-genre did not stop here: in 1936 the Chauvels wrote the screenplay for *Rangle River*, a western featuring mixed-race characters, based on a story by the king of cowboy writers, US novelist Zane Gray.

Marginalising Joe

In a genre where the sins of the father (or mother) are often handed down, someone with mixed blood, often referred to as a 'dirty half-breed' in the scripts, is a much-despised character. This was the case in many early Hollywood westerns. Later, Hollywood came to accept that Native Americans could not be used to construct a mythical west in which they were untameable and therefore dispensable. By the 1950s the western had begun to adopt greater authenticity in its representation of Native Americans. By the late 1940s films like Anthony Mann's *Devil's Doorway* and Delmer Daves' *Broken Arrow* broke the mould by placing the Native American predicament at the centre of the narrative. A group of liberal, anti-racist movies followed, culminating in the early 1970s with films such as *Little Big Man* and *A Man Called Horse,* in which authenticity and positive representation became a major critical issue.

Joe is—almost—an example of this trend. He is treated far more sympathetically than any of the full-blood Indigenous characters (apart from Jedda) and he plays a significant role in the plot—there would not be much of a chase without him. He does not, however, play a central role. Although the narration throughout the film is his, the story never is. This is strange, for according to cinematic conventions, as the narrator, Joe ought to be centre of agency. This is one of the functions of a voice-over narrator: the tale they tell is their story and they are therefore at the centre. But not Joe. True, he gets the first and last words, but he is always at the margins of the story.

Joe's remarkable English accent is what first raised my suspicion that he is in the wrong place. The actual reason for his and the other bizarre accents throughout the film, is mundane: the voices were dubbed on during post-production in England. Despite this, there remains something shady about Joe—played by a white man in dark, if not blackface, he literally pales beside the Indigenous actors. He never has the centrality that by rights, or cinematic convention, should be his.

Inter-racial love

Trying to figure out how and where to locate Joe, a mixed-race man in love with an Indigenous young woman, alerted me to a major silence in *Jedda* concerning inter-racial sexual love. Joe, the 'half-caste', loves Jedda, a love that grows the more assimilated she becomes. But because of her black heart and soul Jedda cannot

A mixed race man in love with an Indigenous woman.

love Joe. When Marbuk breaks his tribe's unbreakable law, he does so with a woman who, although the 'wrong skin', is nevertheless fully Indigenous. In the twisted logic of the narrative's racial politics, if Joe can love Jedda but never make love with her, it is because he is coded as 'white'.

Miscegenation was a controversial topic in 1950s Australia, as it was in the US, and the films of the time reflect this. Although white Australia's policy towards Indigenous people was about 'producing a "new" race from the mixture of Aboriginal and European stock', as Mudrooroo (writing as Colin Johnson) explains, there was nevertheless a widespread fear, especially in the Northern Territory, where Indigenous peoples were in the majority, that the white population 'might lose its place of dominance and be replaced by a "Coloured" majority'.

Novelists were less reluctant to confront the possibility of mixed-race love and sex than filmmakers. At the time of *Jedda*'s release, the reviewer in *The Age* thought the plot was 'derived in essence from Katherine Susannah Pritchard's *Coonardoo*'. Published in 1929, this novel has many similarities with *Jedda*. In it, the white station owner's widow, Mrs Bessie, adopts Coonardoo, a young Aboriginal girl child. Over the years, love blossoms between Coonardoo and Hughie, the white heir to the station. Like Jedda, Coonardoo cannot escape her primaeval nature and ends up 'belonging' to a 'primitive' Aboriginal man. One passage in particular sounds very *Jedda*-like:

> Mrs Bessie realised that though she might teach and train Coonardoo in the ways of a white woman, teach her to cook and sew, be clean and tidy, she would always be an aborigine of the aborigines ... She did not wish to lose Coonardoo. Her people did not wish to lose Coonardoo either. She was theirs by blood and bone, and they were weaving her to the earth and to themselves, through all her senses, appetites and instincts.

There is a significant difference between *Coonardoo* and *Jedda*. In the novel mixed-race love-making, or miscegenation, takes place; in the film it does not. Why not?

Unspoken, unrepresented

Following this line of investigation, I turned to Xavier Herbert's *Capricornia*, another hugely popular and outspoken novel that deals frankly with inter-racial sexual relations. In the following passage, white white-collar worker Mark Shillingworth reveals to his mate, Jock, that he (Mark) is the father of a bastard boy, Norman ('Nawmin' in the novel's demotic language), whose mother is an Aboriginal woman:

> [Mark] had thought of sending Nawmin to the Native Compound in Port Zodiac. He had thought of doing so for years whenever his conscience was pricked by the thought of the boy's growing up as a savage. He had been prevented by the fear that the Protector of Aborigines might discover that he was the father of the child and charge him with the cost of his maintenance.
>
> 'I could do wi' him if ye dawn't wawnt him,' said Jock … 'I've got one yeller-feller meself. Boot it's a bluidy gurrl. I wawnt boys'. He laughed. He went on, 'I wawnt yeller kids to train as foremen. The Government cawn't mairk a bloke pay wages to his own soons – see?'

This helped me see Joe in a very different light. I could now see that he is whiter than Doug McMann would like us—or Sarah— to know, or that Chauvel is prepared to reveal. I'm not the only one to have suspicions about Joe's true parentage. In an article entitled 'Chauvel and the centring of the Aboriginal Male in Australian film', Mudrooroo suggests that although Joe states that his father was an Afghan, his being so close to the McManns and raised by Doug

> to be the head stockman, leads us to believe otherwise, that is the station owner who is in fact the natural father. Chauvel who travelled widely through the outback must have been aware of the sexual exploitation of black females, but he does not allow this to intrude into his films.

This solves the enigma of Joe for me. The absence at the heart of *Jedda* points to an act of miscegenation that the film cannot discuss or represent. To express it publicly would have been unacceptable in a 1950s feature film aiming for mainstream audiences at home and overseas. It would also have challenged very publicly a founding myth of white Australian society. While both the earlier novels directly confront the issue of sex and race, Australia's national cinema was not yet ready to address the issue of miscegenation between the original owners of the land and the white settlers.[22]

VI
CONCLUSION

Assimilation versus 'apartness'

Jedda was made at a time when the issue of where Indigenous peoples fitted in society was being debated throughout Australia.[23] Sarah's views reflect those of the Minister for Territories, Paul Hasluck, whose Liberal/Country Party government had, in 1951, introduced 'assimilation' as official Commonwealth policy. When Sarah insists that Jedda learns her ABC and uses her rolling pin to erase the animal tracks the child has planted in the dough, the film is visualising Hasluck's strong belief that the eventual entry of Indigenous peoples into the white Australian society on equal terms was 'incompatible with full and active preservation of their languages and culture'. Unlike many at the time, Hasluck did not believe assimilation implied racial inter-marriage and biological absorption. Nor did Sarah: raising Jedda to be 'like my own daughter', she did not want her to mate with any of the 'naked monkeys' to whom she was no more like 'than day is to night.'

Doug, on the other hand, believes separatism is preferable to the destruction of Indigenous culture. He is a mouthpiece for the views of influential anthropologist A.P. Elkin (who recorded the film's Indigenous music). In 1944, Elkin had, controversially, called for a 'positive policy which aims at the welfare and development of the aborigines', in a challenge to the widespread view that it was just a matter of time before the whole race died out. Insisting upon the term 'apartness' rather than apartheid, Elkin believed that eventually Indigenous people could be given citizenship, and that this was compatible with the preservation of their cultural identity and distinctiveness.

Chauvel's own views were probably closer to Elkin's than to Hasluck's, as his daughter, Susannah Carlsson, later wrote:

> In *Jedda* Chauvel had attempted to make a simple plea for empathy on behalf of Australian Aborigines, for whom he had sincere respect. He believed that they and their needs were misunderstood, and that they should not be catapulted into the framework of a conventional white society, for which they were not prepared.

Then there are the views of the film itself, about which audiences and critics have to decide for themselves. For some, the film is even-handed because Sarah and Doug express their opposing views cogently and get equal time. For others, the scene of Marbuk's peaceful, if angry, law-giving tribe seems to be offering evidence for the view that no contact at all between the First Nation peoples and the white settlers is the way forward. And then there are those who find that by killing off the two leading characters, the film says assimilation will not work, education is pointless and, left to themselves, and Indigenous people will die out.

This is largely my view (though I hope I have made it clear that I find the film is so much more than just this): the film's greatest flaw is that we never hear an Indigenous viewpoint. It is not that I expect a film of this period to do this but it's an absence that makes it difficult for me to truly love *Jedda*.

The Darwin premiere

>While the guests passed through the foyer with its dazzling
>lights, Robert Tudawali, the star of the film, leaned against the
>front of the cinema unnoticed. When they had gone to their
>seats, Tudawali took his full-blooded wife by the hand and
>went in. The 200 guests and others who had bought tickets
>watched the performance from upstairs but Tudawali and his
>wife sat downstairs. He had been asked where he would like to
>sit and he had said 'Downstairs'. But as he watched the guests
>arrive last night he said, 'I am sorry I am not going upstairs
>with my wife. I should have asked. But as natives normally sit
>downstairs anyway it doesn't matter.'

Almost half a century later, the *Northern Territory News* gave
the story a different slant, this time placing it inside the film's
arguments about assimilation and the white civilising hand.
Robert Tudawali was

>publicly demonstrating that he was an Aborigine and would
>remain one despite official hopes that he would be an early
>and spectacular example of successful Aboriginal assimilation
>and achievement in the white world.[24]

At the time, Rosalie Kunoth's mind was on other matters. Not
fully grasping the film's plot while it was being made because it
was filmed out of sequence, she only understood the implications
of what she had been directed to do at the premiere. Irritated by
Jedda's passivity, during the chase she kept saying to herself, 'She's
stupid, she should run now.' She was also acutely distressed by
the scene which she suddenly realised represented a sexual act,
commenting later, 'The first thing that came into my head was
"what's Mum going to think?"' According to her people's law, she
was not allowed to talk to or look at a strange man, but during

filming she had been made to raise her head and look at Tudawali. She felt deeply ashamed that the Chauvels 'slowly broke my law to make me act'.

Mixed reviews

Although Elsa Chauvel wrote that the film showed to packed theatres throughout Australia, and national pride was justly stroked when it was selected for the Cannes Film Festival, not all reviewers raved about *Jedda*. For those who did, it was generally the film's unique 'Australianness' that was most admired. *Film Weekly* considered it a 'big box-office' movie because it was 'something completely different' and a film that 'could only have been made in Australia'. Like many others, this reviewer also thought it remarkable that Indigenous people could act, commenting that the 'casting is revolutionary: two Australian aborigines in a £100,000 gamble on their ability to act'.

The landscape, the cinematography and the colours of the new Gevacolor film stock did not go unnoticed. Describing the scenery as 'typical Namatjira country', the *Bulletin*'s reviewer and several others echoed the film's own equation of the Indigenous people with the land. Applauding *Jedda* for its 'comely chocolate heroine', 'black hero-villain' and 'dramatic landscapes', *The Age* thought it put on film the 'remote, virtually uncharted regions and peoples of northern Australia not as museum curiosities, but as living human beings'. The *Newsweekly* reviewer felt that the lead actors' performances were less a matter of acting skill than of their 'natural' Aboriginal essence, writing that they had 'the instinctive sense of the dramatic so characteristic of their race'. This essentialist belief was echoed by the *Weekly Times*, which stated that they were 'like most Australian natives ... born mimics', and the London *Times*, whose reviewer thought Tudawali 'emerges as a strong screen personality ... through sheer animal magnificence'.

After Cannes, film posters proclaimed, '*Jedda* wins praise at famed Cannes Film Festival – world's most important and distinguished film exhibition', and quoted from an unnamed reviewer that the film 'drew praise and much favourable comment'. Understandably, the Chauvels' publicity department ignored the prestigious intellectual film journal, *Cahiers du Cinéma*, which condemned 'the incredible puerility of the situations, dialogue and *découpage* [editing technique]' and 'the truly prodigious hideousness of the colour'.

While Australian critics at the time and since—myself included—have insisted on locating *Jedda* in one or more Hollywood genres, in the US, where the film's title was changed to *Jedda the Uncivilised*, several critics did not know what to make of it. The *New York Times* reviewer was frankly baffled. Writing that Jedda ran off with 'a weird-looking tribal barbarian' for 'some rather obscure reason', he failed to grasp why she would have wanted to exchange a happy future with Joe for Marbuk, who was such a 'frightening specimen'. (At this, my heart aches for Robert Tudawali, whose portrayal of Marbuk I find so fine.) Still in the US, the *Box Office Booking Guide* noted the locationism but suggested that this was not all that might interest US audiences:

> An unusual documentary-type drama about the Aborigine territory of northern Australia, this is offbeat fare best suited to the art houses, although the ferocious half-naked savages can be exploited in downtown key city spots.

Individual critics' responses to the film's arguments for and against assimilation were predictable, reflecting the politics of the journal for which they wrote. *Dawn*, a magazine for Indigenous people funded by the NSW government, praised *Jedda* for instilling racial pride. The leftist magazine *Overland*, on the other hand, thought it 'thoroughly bad' and noted that in addition to being 'technically and artistically third-rate [it] peddles the worst kind of racist nonsense'.

No single reading

While many critics, academics and reviewers have written about *Jedda* since it was first released, Stuart Cunningham gives the only detailed analysis in the context of Chauvel's other films and the Australian national cinema as a whole. He argues convincingly that to criticise the film for its naivety and racism is simplistic, and asks us not to ignore:

> the systematic *staging* of conflicting positions that reflects a desire on Chauvel's part to document and narrativise a full range of Aboriginal cultural spaces ... and to maintain the disparity and inadequacy of both central positions – the crude version of assimilationism and of cultural integrity espoused by Sarah and Doug McMann respectively.

Mudrooroo admires the film for different reasons. He sees *Jedda* as an Aboriginal text, commenting that the film is unlike other colonial films such as the *Tarzan* movies because 'The "natives" are not relegated to a romantic backdrop, but are allowed to be centred in the film.' For him, the film invites audiences to sympathise with Jedda and Marbuk. He notes that Marbuk was at that time the only dignified Aboriginal male lead in a film made by a white director, and although he eventually dies, he does so because he has offended his own law rather than because of anything the white man has done to him. Mudrooroo sees

Jedda's 'very passivity' as reflecting 'the passivity of adolescent black girls locked up in mission compounds, thick with stories of savage myalls prowling the fence of the compound ready to steal them away'.

For Indigenous scholar and actor Marcia Langton, however, the film is nothing but 'a colonialist fantasy' masking the truth of frontier brutality in melodrama. In an essay 'by and about Aboriginal people and things' she argues: 'It rewrites Australian history so that the black rebel against white colonial rule is a rebel against the laws of his own society.' For her, Jedda and Marbuk's deaths visualise the widespread ideological belief of the period that the Aborigines were 'dying out'. This, she argues, was a highly convenient notion in a society committed to pioneer legends and which had not yet confronted the facts of invasion, dispossession, dislocation and relocation.

Perhaps the film's continuing attraction for many Indigenous and non-Indigenous audiences has to do with Marbuk's dominance, which affirms the power of Aboriginal culture over white civilisation. In short, there is no single Indigenous reading of the film, just as there is no single non-Indigenous reading.

I know that the film—like any film—is open to multiple readings which may have little or nothing to do with what the filmmakers intend. But I cannot avoid seeing what I think are the filmmakers' own political beliefs. These I find racist. This does not mean that I ignore or discount what critic Paul Byrnes describes as the film's 'unusual degree of sympathy for, and interest in, Aboriginal culture'. I can also appreciate how the film offers more perspectives on Aboriginality and a wider range of Indigenous lives than most films and other works of fiction and documentary did then and now.

Ultimately, however, I can see no way round the fact that the film comes down on the side of Doug's position, which Cunningham bluntly names 'benevolent apartheid'. That Jedda and Marbuk are both killed off says to me that the film holds out no hope of a black-white intercultural future for Australia. I cannot accept the argument that I am imposing 21st century ideas upon a film from another time, another place. As Henry Reynolds' book, *This Whispering in our Hearts*, tells us, there have been Australians opposed to the destruction of Indigenous rights and who argued for interculturalism between Black and White Australians since the late 18th century. There were most certainly Australians in the 1950s who opposed the government's assimilationist policy, who were appalled by Hasluck's belief that 'the weakness of the old Aboriginal society ... is an advantage. The more it crumbles, the more readily may its fragments be mingled with the rest of the people living in Australia', and who strongly disagreed with Elkin's perception of Aborigines as a primitive people with a smaller-sized brain. But in *Jedda* there is no place for Indigenous viewpoints.

An enduring presence

Jedda continues to be important in Australian cultural life precisely because of how and what it tells us about racial politics then and now. Most recently, it infiltrated Baz Luhrmann's film *Australia* as one of its many intertextual references: the Drover's dog in *Australia* is named 'Jedda'; the lead white female character in both films is named 'Sarah'; the narrators are both mixed-race; and the issue of assimilation through the adoption of an Aboriginal (or part-Aboriginal) child by a white couple lies at the heart of both narratives. As academics Peta Mitchell and Jane Stadler point out, *Australia* is a 're-visioning' of *Jedda*.

Of all critical engagements with *Jedda*, the most eloquent is surely Indigenous filmmaker Tracey Moffatt's short film, *Night Cries: A Rural Tragedy*. This extraordinarily moving avant-garde film of the late1980s shows us what might have happened had *Jedda* not plunged to her death from that cliff top, and had Sarah not been written out of the script halfway through. We see an old—ancient, really—white mother (Agnes Hardwick), crippled, confined to a wheelchair and possibly suffering from dementia. She is locked in a bitter relationship of co-dependency with her middle-aged Aboriginal adopted daughter (Marcia Langton), her sole carer. Taking an inspired approach to Chauvel's locationism, *Night Cries* is filmed entirely in a studio set designed by Stephen Curtis that uncannily evokes the set for the Mongala Station kitchen and the beautiful tones of Namatjira's landscapes.

Responding to the questions Jedda poses about assimilation, Moffatt's film sees the two races as inseparable; the mutual dependency created by a shared heritage is unbreakable. Her vision for what might become of the relationship between Black and White Australians is not a happy one: *Night Cries* ends with both mother and daughter in tears. Assimilation, the film implies, causes pain to both the Aboriginal child and the white parent because no one has worked out that the parent-child relationship is out of place. Suggesting that there is an emotional as well as an intellectual gap between the two peoples, this powerful film leaves its audiences to ponder how the gap might be filled. Reconciliation, anyone?

Watching *Night Cries* and its remarkable set design made me return to *Jedda*, to watch it once again. This time, the images of land and landscape showed me not only that Chauvel loved Australia, but how much he loved it. What also struck me in this particular viewing was Namatjira's influence on the film's landscape images. This, I think, offers a glimpse of the film's respect for just how much Australia's First Nation peoples also love the land, their land, and have done so for very many more years than anyone else.

ENDNOTES

1   I was also travelling in the footsteps of a fellow film academic and friend, Jane Stadler, who visited *Jedda*'s Northern Territory locations and, like me, is fascinated by the relationship between cinema and geography.

2   'Lubra', meaning 'woman', is from a Tasmanian Indigenous language. The term is now considered racially offensive.

3   Upon marrying Bill Monks in 1970, Rosalie Kunoth changed her last name to Kunoth-Monks.

4   Charles and Elsa Chauvel's daughter, Susanne Chauvel Carlsson, remembers her father having warm friendships with many Indigenous people in the Northern Territory, including Albert Namatjira. In *My Life with Charles Chauvel*, Elsa Chauvel includes a photo of a young Susanne sketching Namatjira at Hermannsburg, a small mission community west of Alice Springs.

5   It has long been thought that the final scene was originally filmed in Katherine Gorge— presumably at the rock now known as Jedda's Leap. The rushes were supposedly destroyed in a plane crash on their way to the laboratories in the UK, thus forcing Chauvel to reshoot the scene closer to Sydney. However, Chauvel's grandson, Ric Chauvel Carlsson, tells me that he and his mother, Susanne Chauvel Carlsson, have found an earlier screenplay which suggests there was no plane crash and that the final death scene was only added much later, after the crew had left the Northern Territory.

6   Not long after *Jedda*, Rosalie Kunoth-Monks became an Anglican nun. After leaving the convent several years later she became a social worker for Indigenous communities, then a political activist, standing as a candidate for the Country Liberal Party in the Northern Territory seat of Macdonnell. She is now a highly respected Elder, living with her family in the community of Utopia, where she was born.

7   To learn more about Australian cinema, there's no better place than Tom O'Regan's book, *Australian National Cinema* (1996).

8   The first colour film ever shot in Australia was the 1952 Hollywood movie, *Kangaroo*, starring Hollywood actors Peter Lawford and Maureen O'Hara. Australian actors Chips Rafferty and Charles 'Bud' Tingwell also appear. Despite

reportedly earning £2000 a week, O'Hara refused to join the Communist-led actors' union, which successfully prevented the Aboriginal extras being paid less than white ones. The two speaking parts for Aboriginal characters are played by white actors in blackface.

9   See: http://aso.gov.au/titles/features/jedda/

10 The Arrernte peoples' traditional land is in central Australia, around Alice Springs and the Western and Eastern Macdonnell Ranges. They are also referred to as Aranda, Arrarnta, Arunta, and other similar spellings.

11 I find genre theory fascinating, if complex, because it looks at the relationship between what's happening on the screen and what's going on in the audience's mind. For a helpful introduction to this and other aspects of film theory Susan Hayward's *Cinema Studies: The Key Concepts* is invaluable.

12 Elsa disliked the bachelor owner of Coolibah Station as this extract from her book reveals: 'He was a rough-hewn man, moody and aggressive … He told of the good old bad days and the general treatment meted out to offending aborigines who slacked in their work, or were caught with a stolen tin of jam under their shirts. He made no effort to deny his own part in the punishment, which if it were true, measured up well to that handed out to the early slaves in America.'

13 This comment of Sarah's perplexed me for some years. Surely a newborn baby would stand greater chance of surviving if it were breastfed as soon as possible? The reason is probably less suspicious than I originally thought. While Dr Benjamin Spock's widely read book, *Baby and Child Care*, recommended breastfeeding, it also stated that bottle-feeding was acceptable. As formula milk was considered more 'modern' than breast milk in the 1950s, I now think that Sarah, who considered herself a progressive Southerner (rather as did the Victorian Jeannie Gunn of *We of the Never Never*), would have bought some formula milk for her own baby and so found a use for it when Jedda arrived.

14 Young Joe, played by Willie Farrar, is another example of Chauvel's interweaving of fact into his fiction in order to achieve greater 'authenticity'. He cast this rather solemn little

boy because his grandfather had been a trail-blazing head musterer for some of the early white pioneers in the region.

15 The kinship system is a feature of Aboriginal social organisation and family relationships. It determines how people relate to each other and their roles, responsibilities and obligations in relation to one another, ceremonial business and land. Today, the number of 'wrong skin' marriages is increasing, and families are attempting to accommodate the contradictions.

16 Jedda would probably never have heard of the wompoo pigeon, or fruit dove, which is a rainforest fruit bird found only in the eastern regions of Queensland and northern New South Wales.

17 Idriess refers to Nemarluk as the 'last of the Stone Age men', but as the publishers justly claim, *Nemarluk: King of the Wilds* was 'one of the few books written from a sympathetic perspective at a time when few white writers had the experience or understanding to tackle stories about Aborigines. It is not only a fast-moving tale about heroism but also an important document

recording the social and ethical relationships between black and white Australians.'

18 For a thoughtful analysis of how the notion of 'imaginative geography' relates to *Jedda*, see Peta Mitchell and Jane Stadler's article.

19 Darlene Johnson's documentary, *The Stolen Generations*, offers good evidence of the connection between anthropology, filmmaking and white colonial rule in Australia.

20 Stuart Cunningham compares *Jedda* with Hollywood melodramas such as *All that Heaven Allows, The Reckless Moment, Some Came Running, The Bad and the Beautiful* and *Written on the Wind.*

21 Cultural geographer Tim Cresswell argues that ideas about what is right, just, and appropriate are transmitted through space and place.

22 John Ford's classic western, *The Searchers*, made one year before *Jedda*, is another film in which miscegenation cannot be named. It is a fear that dominates almost every waking thought of Ethan (John Wayne) but is absent from his vocabulary. Finding a niece killed and presumably raped by the Comanche, all Ethan can say to the young 'half-caste' Martin

Pawley (Jeffrey Hunter) who wants to know what happened is: 'I thought it best to keep it from you...What do you want me to do, draw you a picture?... As long as you live don't ever ask me that.'

23 For further discussion of these ideas, see the articles referenced in the back of this book by Anthony Moran, Russell McGregor, Jeremy Beckett, and A.P. Elkin's 1944 booklet, *Citizenship for the Aborigines: A National Aboriginal Policy Statement*.

24 After *Jedda*, Tudawali was allocated a house in a white suburb, but after a few months he asked to move back to an Indigenous suburb. In 1956, after national newspapers reported that he was destitute and suffering from tuberculosis, Minister for Territories Paul Hasluck was criticised in the Commonwealth parliament for the failure of the Territory's Welfare Branch to protect Tudawali's interests. After a couple of roles in a minor film, *Dust in the Sun* (1958), and the television series *Whiplash*, he drifted in and out of hospital and gaol for repeated offences against liquor laws. In 1963, the Welfare Branch banished him to Melville Island for nine months. In 1966, he was elected Vice-president of the Northern Territory Council

for Aboriginal Rights and he supported the Aboriginal stockmen's strike. He died of severe burns and tuberculosis on 26 July 1967. See *Australian Dictionary of Biography* at http://adb.anu.edu.au/biography/tudawali-robert-11889.

BIBLIOGRAPHY

Books, articles and interviews cited and consulted

Beckett, Jeremy, "Sarah McMahon's Mistake: Charles Chauvel's Jedda and the Assimilation Policy." *The Olive Pink Society Bulletin*. 5 (2). Dec 1993

Byrnes, Paul, *Jedda*: Curator's Notes. Australian Screen. http://aso.gov.au/titles/features/jedda/notes/

Carlsson, Susanne Chauvel, *Charles and Elsa Chauvel: Movie Pioneers*. Brisbane: University of Queensland Press, 1989

Chauvel, Charles and Elsa, *Walkabout*. London: W.H. Allen, 1959

Chauvel, Elsa, *My Life with Charles Chauvel*. Sydney: Shakespeare Press, 1973

Columbia Pictures, *Eve in Ebony ... the story of* "Jedda". Sydney, 1954

Connor, Liz, '"Strangely clad": Enclosure, exposure, and the cleavage of empire'. *Journal of Australian Studies*, 35 (2), 2011

Creed, Barbara. 'Breeding out the Black: *Jedda* and the Stolen Generations in Australia', in Barbara Creed and Jeannette Hoorn (eds), *Body Trade: Captivity, Cannibalism and Colonialism in the Pacific*, New York: Routledge, 2002

Creed, Barbara, '*Jedda*, Négritude and the Modernist Impulse in Australian Film', in Robert Dixon and Veronica Kelly (eds), *Impact of the Modern: Vernacular Modernities in Australia 1870s–1960s*, Sydney: Sydney University Press, 2008

Cresswell, Tim, *In Place/Out of Place: Geography, Ideology and Transgression*, Minneapolis MN: University of Minnesota Press, 1996

Cunningham, Stuart, *Featuring Australia: The Cinema of Charles Chauvel*, Sydney: Allen & Unwin, 1991

Dawn, '*Jedda* is YOUR Film.' 3 (9),1954

Denton, Andrew. 'Elders with Andrew Denton: Rosalie Kunoth Monks', Episode 5, ABC Television, 14 December 2009

Elkin, A,P, *Citizenship for the Aborigines: A National Aboriginal Policy Statement*, Sydney, 1944

Fox, Karen, 'Rosalie Kunoth-Monks and the making of *Jedda*'. *Aboriginal History*, 33, 2009

Gunn, Mrs Aeneas [Jeannie], *We of the Never Never & The Little Black Princess*, [1905], Sydney: Angus & Robertson, 1982

Hayward, Susan, *Cinema Studies: The Key Concepts*, (3rd edition), London: Routledge, 2010

Herbert, Xavier, *Capricornia*, [1938], Sydney: HarperCollins, 1985

Hoorn, Jeanette, 'White lubra/white savage: Pituri and colonialist fantasy in Charles Chauvel's *Uncivilised* (1936)', *Post Script*, vol. 24 nos 2–3, 2005

Hughes, Robin, Interview with Rosalie Kunoth-Monks, July 2005, http://www.australianbiography.gov.au/subjects/kunothmonks

Idriess, Ion, *Nemarluk: King of the Wilds*, Sydney: Angus & Robertson, 1941

Jennings, Karen, *Sites of Difference: Cinematic Representations of Aboriginallity*, Melbourne: AFI, 1993

Johnson, Colin [Mudrooroo Nyoongah], 'Chauvel and the centring of the Aboriginal male in Australian film', *Continuum: The Australian Journal of Media & Culture*, vol. 1, no. 1, 1987

Kaplan, E. Ann, 'Aborigines, Film and Moffatt's Night Cries: A Rural Tragedy: An Outsider's Perspective', *The Olive Pink Society Bulletin*, 2 (1), 1989

Lambert, Anthony, 'Arresting Metaphors: Anti-Colonial Females in Australian Cinema', *Postcolonial Text*, 1 (2), 2005

Langton, Marcia. '"Well, I heard it on the radio and I saw it on the television ..." An essay for the Australian Film Commission by and about Aboriginal people and things', Sydney: AFI, 1993

Lawson, Sylvia. 'Out of the Mid-Century: History, Memory and Cinema', Lola.1, 2011, http://www.lolajournal.com/1/midcentury.html

Lefevbre, Martin, 'Between Setting and Landscape in the Cinema', in Martin Lefevbre (ed.), *Landscape and Film*, New York: Routledge, 2006

Limbrick, Peter, 'The Australian Western, or A Settler Colonial Cinema par excellence', *Cinema Journal*, 46 (4), 2007

McGregor, Russell, 'Intelligent Parasitism: A.P. Elkin and the Rhetoric of Assimilation.' *Journal of Australian Studies*, 20 (50-51), 1996

Miller, Benjamin, 'The Mirror of Whiteness: Blackface in Charles Chauvel's *Jedda*', *JASAL*, Special issue, 2007

Mitchell, Peta and Stadler, Jane, 'Imaginative Cinematic Geographies of Australia: The Mapped View in Charles Chauvel's *Jedda* and Baz Luhrmann's *Australia*', *Historical Geography*, 38, 2010

Moran, Anthony, 'White Australia, Settler Nationalism and Aboriginal Assimilation.' *Australian Journal of Politics and History*, 51 (2), 2005

Mudrooroo, Nyoongah (Narogin), 'Introduction' in Xavier Herbert, *Capricornia*, [1938], Sydney: HarperCollins, 1990 (See also Colin Johnson)

O'Regan, Tom, *Australian National Cinema*, London: Routledge, 1996

Pike, Andrew, 'Aboriginals in Australian Feature Films', *Meanjin*, vol. 36, no. 4, 1977

Pritchard, Katherine Susannah, *Coonardoo*, [1929], Sydney: Angus & Robertson, 1986

Probyn-Rapsey, Fiona, 'Some Whites are Whiter Than Others: The Whitefella Skin Politics of Xavier Herbert and Cecil Cook. *JASAL Special Issue*, 2007

Reynolds, Henry, *This Whispering in our Hearts*, Crows Nest: Allen & Unwin, 1998

Said, Edward, *Orientalism*. New York: Vintage, 1979

Schlunke, Katrina, 'Imaging the Imagined: Stories of *Jedda*', *The Olive Pink Society Bulletin*, 5 (2), 1993

Shaw, Bruce, 'Nemarluk (1911–1940)', *Australian Dictionary of Biography*, National Centre of Biography, Australian National University at http://adb.anu.edu.au/biography/nemarluk-11222/text20009.

Tulloch, John, *Legends on the Screen: Australian Narrative Cinema 1912*, Sydney: Currency Press/AFI, 1981

FILMS & TELEVISION

All that Heaven Allows, Douglas Sirk, 1955

amant L'/The Lover, Jean-Jaques Annaud, 1992

Australia, Baz Luhrmann, 2008

Australian Walkabout, Charles & Elsa Chauvel, 1958 (13 eps, BBC Television)

Bad and the Beautiful, The, Vincente Minnelli, 1952

Battle for Algiers, The, Gillo Pontecorvo, 1968

Birth of a Nation, D.W. Griffith, 1915

Birth of White Australia, Phil Walsh, 1928

Chant of Jimmie Blacksmith, The,. Fred Schepisi, 1978

Duel In The Sun, King Vidor, 1946

Greenhide, Charles Chauvel, 1926

Gunga Din, George Stevens, 1939

Little Big Man, Arthur Penn, 1970

Man Called Horse, A, Elliot Silverstein, 1970

Moth of Moonbi, The, Charles Chauvel, 1926

Night Cries: A Rural Tragedy, Tracey Moffatt, 1989

Olympia, Leni Riefenstahl, 1938

Overlanders, The, Harry Watts, 1946

Rangle River, Clarence G. Badger, 1936

Reckless Moment, The, Max Ophuls, 1949

Sanders of the River, Zoltan Korda, 1935

Searchers, The, John Ford, 1956

Some Came Running, Vincente Minnelli, 1958

Song of Ceylon, A. Laleen Jayamanne, 1985

Song of Ceylon, Basil Wright, 1934

Sons of Matthew, Charles Chauvel, 1949

Stolen Generations, Darlene Johnson, 2000

Triumph of the Will, Leni Riefenstahl, 1934

Uncivilised, Charles Chauvel, 1936

Written on the Wind, Douglas Sirk, 1956

CREDITS

Release year
1955

Production Company
Charles Chauvel Productions

Key crew

Producer, Director
Charles Chauvel

Screenplay
Charles Chauvel, Elsa Chauvel

Director of Photography
Carl Keyser

Special photography
Eric Porter

Dialogue Direction
Elsa Chauvel

Editors
Alex Ezard, Jack Gardiner,
Pam Bosworth

Sound
Arthur Browne

Assistant Director
Philip Pike

Unit Manager
Harry Closter

Technician
Tex Foote

Original music, conductor
Isadore Goodman

Song: 'Dreamtime for Jedda'
Leslie Lewis Raphael

Song recorded by
Bob Gibson

Vocals
Jimmy Parkinson

Special Aboriginal recording
Professor Elkin

Research
Bill Harney

Costumes
Wendels

Key cast

Jedda
Narla [Ngarla] Kunoth
[Real name: Rosalie Kunoth, later
Kunoth-Monks]

Marbuk Robert Tudewalli
[Tudawali] [Real name:
Robert Wilson]

Sarah McMann
Betty Suttor

'Joe' (half caste)
Paul Reynall [Real name: Paul Clarke]

Douglas McMann
George Simpson-Lyttle

Police Officer
Peter Wallis

**Tas Fitzer of the Northern
Territory Mounted Police**

Felix Romeo (boss drover)
Wason Byers

Little Joe
Willie Farrar

Little Jedda
Margaret Dingle

Nosepeg
Tjunkata Tjupurrula (uncredited)

Aborigines of the Pitjantjara, Aranda,
Pintubi, Yungman, Djauan, Waugits,
and Tiwi tribes of north and central
Australia.

Uncredited Indigenous actors in
directed roles with the names
of Moonlight, Charcoal, Booloo,
Millie, May, Nita, Bessie and others
unnamed.

A 'full-blood outlaw from the Tiwi tribe'.

A 'hybrid western melodrama'.

A ponderous Jedda.

Happier times.

The AUSTRALIAN SCREEN CLASSICS is now a subscription series!

To subscribe please go to our website:

www.currency.com.au

Other titles in the series include:

The Adventures of Priscilla, Queen of the Desert by Philip Brophy
ISBN 978 0 86819 821 7
In his provocative reading of Stephan Elliott's cult 1994 film, Philip Brophy invites us to think more deeply about what this film is saying about Australia, its history, its culture and its cinema.

Alvin Purple by Catharine Lumby
ISBN 978 0 86819 844 6
Australia's first R-rated feature film created a furore when it was released in 1973. Catharine Lumby revisits claims that the movie is an exercise in sexploitation and argues the films complexity.

The Barry McKenzie Movies by Tony Moore
ISBN 978 0 86819 748 7
An illuminating tribute to Bruce Beresford's subversive and hilarious *The Adventures of Barry McKenzie*, and its riotous sequel, by cultural historian and documentary-filmmaker, Tony Moore.

The Boys by Andrew Frost
ISBN 978 0 86819 862 0
Andrew Frost's monograph explores the achievements of this award-winning film, placing its thematic concerns into a broader context of social anxieties about violence, crime and morality.

The Chant of Jimmie Blacksmith by Henry Reynolds
ISBN 978 0 86819 824 8
Based on Thomas Keneally's award-winning novel, Fred Schepisi's 1978 film is a powerful and confronting story of a black man's revenge against an injust and intolerant society.

The Devil's Playground by Christos Tsiolkas
ISBN 978 0 86819 671 8
Christos Tsiolkas invites you into Fred Schepisi's haunting film about a thirteen-year-old boy struggling with life in a Catholic seminary. ww

The Mad Max Movies by Adrian Martin
ISBN 978 0 86819 670 1
Adrian Martin offers a new appreciation of these classics: *'No other Australian films have influenced world cinema and popular culture as widely and lastingly as George Miller's Mad Max movies'.*

The Piano by Gail Jones
ISBN 978 0 86819 799 9
Writer Gail Jones' thoughtful and perceptive critique of Jane Campion's award-winning film, *The Piano*, assesses the film's controversial visions, poetic power and capacity to alienate.

Puberty Blues by Nell Schofield
ISBN 978 0 86819 749 4
'Fish-faced moll', 'rooting machine', 'melting our tits off': with its raw dialogue, Bruce Beresford's *Puberty Blues* has become a cult classic. Nell Schofield takes a look at this much-loved film.

Wake in Fright by Tina Kaufman
ISBN 978 0 86819 864 4
Tina Kaufman's essay explores how *Wake in Fright* was received on its first release in 1971. She also discusses the film's discovery after being lost for over a decade and its second release in 2009.

Walkabout by Louis Nowra
ISBN 978 0 86819 700 5
Louis Nowra says *Walkabout* 'destroyed the cliché of the Dead Heart and made us Australians see it from a unique perspective'.

'The Australian Screen Classics series is surely a must for any Australian film buff's library'
Phillip King, Royal Holloway, University of London

'The Australian Screen Classics series provides an invaluable space for the examination, celebration and critique of our national film heritage'
Real Time

Available from all good bookshops or buy online at
www.currency.com.au